Cast
Your Bread
Upon
The Waters

Cast Your Bread Upon The Waters

**Personal Experiences
of the Biblical Promise
"Cast your bread
upon the waters, for you
will find it
after many days."**

Ruth Youngdahl Nelson
with her husband Clarence T. Nelson

AUGSBURG PUBLISHING HOUSE
MINNEAPOLIS, MINNESOTA

CAST YOUR BREAD UPON THE WATERS

MANUFACTURED IN THE UNITED STATES OF AMERICA

Contents

Preface

In the days when one was free to come and go from mainland China, one Christian sister stopped off in the Philippine
Islands on her return to the States. While visiting friends
there, she was asked to speak in the church. There she described the widespread famine in China and told of hungry
children whose mothers had nothing to feed them and of the
many who died as a result.

In the congregation was an 11-year-old boy whose heart
was deeply touched. For months he had been saving money
to buy a bicycle. This had been the dream of his heart. Now
he had almost enough to buy the model he wanted, nearly
$30, a large amount in the days before inflation.

But he was haunted by the memory of these starving children. He thought of boys like himself, whose stomachs were
in pain for lack of food. Apparently he went through a great
struggle. Was it right that he should have to give up a dream
of owning the bike he had worked for? And yet, those hungry
children were on his heart. And $30 would buy quite a bit of
bread!

That Sunday night his sleep was fitful and he was hollow-
eyed the next morning. His mother asked if he might be ill.

Her intuition told her that something was bothering him, but he was in no mood to vent his feelings. She was anxious for him to return from school and became concerned when he didn't appear at the expected time. When he finally came, he was aglow—and then he told her his story.

He had decided during the night that he could never be happy with the bike because he knew some children could be alive with his money. So he had taken his savings with him to school, and after school hours, he had gone directly to the bakery. There he counted out his money before the wide-eyed baker and said, "Sir, how many loaves of bread would this buy? I want to buy as much bread as I can to send to the hungry children of China."

At first the baker was completely taken aback, but then he said to the boy, "That's a beautiful thing you want to do. Where did you get this money?"

"It's my bicycle money," was his answer, "but I don't really need a bicycle to live, and those Chinese kids need the bread!"

Then the baker explained how that the bread would spoil before it could reach that faraway land. This was before planes spanned the wide waters of the Pacific. But the baker also promised that he would personally talk with the missionary to find a way to send this money to someone in China who could buy the life-giving loaves to feed those starving children.

Well, the baker did more than this! He went to his church people and told them about this boy's sacrificial gift. He challenged them to add theirs to the gift he had set apart. The Lord's multiplication was working. In a short time in this small congregation, $3,500 were raised and sent to responsible people in mainland China for food.

But that isn't the end of the story. A missionary was relating it in a large church in Detroit. After the service, a man came up and said, "Do you have the name and address of that boy? I'd like to write him!" The man who wanted that information was Henry Ford. And Henry Ford followed through. He bought the boy in the Philippines the finest bicycle he could find, and then he sent a sizable donation to China Relief.

You think our story is finished? Well it isn't. The lad was overwhelmed with the gift and wondered how he could use it to make possible still more bread money. He saw how enviously the other boys looked at his bike! So he decided to rent it out for rides, and whatever money came he would add to the fund for hungry Chinese. The multiplication went on and on. Jesus used a lad's lunch of loaves and fishes to feed a Galilean multitude; in the Philippines he used a boy's response to human need to bless many.

It doesn't always happen that the thing you give up is replaced. One doesn't look for that. But when you cast your bread upon the waters, the Lord does return a hundredfold in the deep-down joy of giving.

The pages that follow recount vignettes that witness to the amazing way God takes the "bread" shared with others and multiplies it to enrich the lives of the givers beyond anything they could dream.

In this remembrancing we are concerned about three things: first, that the Lord who gave the opportunities be given all the glory. It is the Lord also who provided the wherewithal! And his Holy Spirit did the nudging. Our regret is that we didn't always respond to his promptings. Second, we are concerned that you do not fall into the trap of thinking that one should always receive a reward. The Lord never promised that. His Word reads rather, "One man sows; another reaps; and God gives the increase!" Our response should be to sow his love and then trust him for the rest.

In some instances we were "taken for a ride" even in the matter of hospitality in our home. We sometimes regretted that we were so gullible. Yet we concluded that we would rather err on the side of generosity than deny help to someone in need.

Our third concern is to emphasize the joy of Christian hospitality. We regret that the grace of home hospitality is sometimes minimized and deprecated, especially by some who have made the full swing to women's lib! Don't misunderstand! We believe that in God's great Book equality is the theme and that anything which downgrades any group of people or any person is not biblical. We also believe that God treats us each as individuals—not according to our sex, or race, or economic or intellectual capacities.

For many of us, life's richest fulfillment comes through sharing our home, in keeping its doors wide open to all people, in practicing Christian hospitality without wishing we didn't have to, in making it a joyous place with windows open to the world. I have been inspired by reading Margaret Wold's *The Shalom Woman.* We do need to be aroused to our potential and our responsibilities in today's world and share this concern with our sisters. But we also need to be launching pads for the love of the Lord to all the world. My experience with this kind of opportunity has been one of irrepressible joy. I could wish more young women would choose to follow a like pattern. In all humility I hope that what we have here written will be a challenge to our great opportunity to bring our gifts, our intuitions, our imagination and our love into our homes.

The God of seed-time and harvest is calling each of us to claim his promise: "Cast your bread upon the waters, and it will return after many days" (Eccles. 11:1). And when it comes to the increase, it seems that God displaces simple multiplication with a geometric piling up of these returns. Mere words get threadbare when we try to convey our gratitude. "Hallelujah," which literally means a "holy hurrah," puts it best.

This isn't "my" book; it is "our" book in more ways than one. My beloved husband has written much of this book and he has also encouraged and helped me in my writing. Even to the time before the writing, it has been our work together, our teamwork that has played a large part in making possible the sharing of the bread. The fact that we were of one mind in this regard made the extra work easy, and somehow the good Lord always provided the wherewithal, scant though our resources were. Which brings me to the basic "our" relationship!

Because we wanted Christ to be the head of our house, because through his Word we sought to know what a Christian home should be like, we were enabled to have an open door into open hearts! The Lord is the most important part of the "our."

The "our" also includes parents who set the example and in whose lives we saw the joy of willing hospitality.

Nor should we forget the children in the "our." They often were the stimulus and the medium through which fascinating opportunities came.

So this is "our" book to the glory of His name and to the wonder of His enabling!

We should like to acknowledge, too, with gratitude, the fine encouragement and cooperation of Augsburg Publishing House.

Most names are real. But some have been changed so as not to embarrass those involved.

It All Began
with Birthday Cakes

Early in our married life we learned the truth of the promise of the hundred-fold return of bread cast upon the waters. The experience really began with birthday cakes.

As a school teacher I had been aware of everyone's need to know that he is somebody, somebody important to God. There were older folks in our parish who seemed to be forgotten people. I thought it would be fun to remember their birthdays, so I asked the church secretary to make a birthday list of everybody over 65. I chuckle when I think of that, because from the vantage point of my years today, 65 seems young!

Believing that butter cakes just weren't good for the aging, I mostly baked egg cakes: angel food (when I had gathered enough egg whites from the egg yokes our babies were fed), or five-egg sunshine cakes, or Mrs. Basil Nelson's hot milk cake. There were no cake mixes in that day. Generally I baked them the day before, and on the morning of the birthday I would frost and decorate them with the recipient's names. I can still hear our little ones, as they listened to the bustle in the kitchen or as they licked the frosting bowl, ask, "Mommy, which grandma's birthday is it today?"

Early afternoon we were off to the home of the birthday

person. What fun that moment of greeting the surprised person, as we came over the threshold singing "Happy Birthday" and put the cake in their hands. I wish I had used a camera! But my mind snapped those pictures and even now as I write, one face after the other is flashed back showing surprised joy. "How could you remember me?" would often be the question. Before we left, Clarence would share a minnesord (i.e., a word of remembrance) and then he would lift up the special person in prayer. We would always sing favorite hymns. The wealthiest person in the world couldn't begin to pay for the joy we knew in those times of sharing.

This time it was Martha Mulvey's turn for the birthday visit. We drove through rolling wooded hills to see 90-year-old Martha in her room at a Maryland nursing home.

Martha had lived a fascinating life. Coming from Sweden in her early teens, she found no difficulty in obtaining domestic work. With natural culinary instinct, she developed into a creative and skillful cook. She met and married an Irishman, Pat Mulvey by name, and although she still worked outside of the home, she was able to tickle his palate and keep him pleased with his choice of a Swedish wife.

How she came to get her first job we never did hear, but rarely did we visit her but what she regaled us with the fact that she had cooked for five presidents in the White House. She loved to recount how William Howard Taft would sometimes come into the White House kitchen to speak his appreciation for some toothsome dish she had prepared. His portly frame was evidence enough that he enjoyed good food.

On one of those visits he even asked, "Martha, are they treating you all right here?" She loved him for being the jolly, loving, human kind of person he was. My husband asked, "What was President Taft's favorite dish?" She replied, "Hog jowl." Wouldn't a French chef turn up his nose at that!

But on this special day of her 90th birthday she reigned like a queen from her wheelchair. We found a folding table and set up the candle birthday ring with the cake in the center. A thoughtful friend had provided this attractive ring just for such occasions. Out came the cardamom coffee bread. My husband wondered at my boldness in daring to serve such a culinary expert my kitchen offerings. But I knew Martha well enough. She would judge it in the light of the love that prompted it. We had coffee in our thermos bottles and were about to open them when she said, "Wait a minute! I have something I want you to read." Then she asked us to reach to her well worn purse, and out of it she drew a letter with the return, "White House." Handing it to me, she said, "It's from Mamie Eisenhower. Please read it, Mrs. Nelson."

In it the President's wife had written that she had come across White House records indicating how Martha had served as chief cook those many years, and so she wanted to send her warm regards on this special birthday! I wish Mrs. Eisenhower could have seen the joy her letter brought to this senior citizen secluded in one of the corners of a city. I did try to describe it to Mamie in a letter of thanks Martha asked me to write.

Everything didn't always turn out that smoothly. Our visit was in spring and the winter ice and snow had caused deep ruts in that twisting road through the woods that led to the nursing home entry. The building itself was a converted mansion of elegance. In some places sharp rocks jutted from the hump between the ruts and one of these had pierced our oil pan causing the oil to run out. The flashing red on the dashboard was our first warning. But by then it was already too late and our pistons were burnt and we ground to a stop. By telephone we arranged for repairs and then called my brother, Judge Luther Youngdahl, for a lift home. When my husband described where we were he retorted, "Say, Clarence, how far into Maryland does your parish extend anyway?" Suffice it to say that the whole experience made that pastoral call unforgettable.

Not too long after that memorable birthday, the Lord gently tapped Martha on the shoulder, bidding her to "step higher up." Then we took inventory of how she had blessed our lives.

The Gift of Emil Welti

One of the most outstanding examples of the hundred-fold return of love given is the story of Emil Welti. His story took place in the years of the great depression, a time that proved to be the most rewarding of our lives. It was rewarding, not in monetary terms as the world counts riches, but in the joy and wealth of being needed. Many times we didn't know where the money for the next grocery bill would come from, but we never really lacked. Those of you who have tried the Lord know how wonderfully he provides. Like the day that strange envelope arrived in the mail!

We really were down to zero, and payday for our meager salary was still two days away. I remember handling that somewhat soiled envelope when the mailman delivered it. There was no return address, no signature to provide a cue. Curiously I opened it. Its contents were indeed strange: two one-dollar bills enclosed in a torn-out page of a Gospel hymnal. The title of the song was, "Hold the Fort, Brother." There had been some dissension in the church about architectural plans to go ahead with the upper structure. What we least needed was a divided house! The congregation had met in a basement for 11 years. A good number of the breadwinners were skilled laborers: carpenters, plumbers, bricklayers, electricians, plasterers. They had been out of work for a long time following the stock market crash in 1929. We were in the trough of the depression. And yet we were hard at completing the plans to get the building up out of the ground. Now arose the threat of two factions splitting the flock. Clarence was in favor of pulling in the walls to avoid the construction of a sanctuary which could be filled only on Easter and Christmas. The architect came up with a plan to put clerestory aisles on either side and to eliminate one of the huge fortress-style towers, thereby reducing considerably the price tag that went with it. But before I get into that story, let me tell you that those two dollars tided us over until the salary check was in hand. And the encouragement of that hymn put fresh starch into my husband. We never did learn whom to thank!

But to get back to the story of Emil Welti. One woman called (not a member). She said, "Pastor, I understand that you often get out to call on the sick in the General Hospital. A little Swiss gentleman who used to be an errand boy in our office is a patient there. He had surgery and is now convalescing. He has no family and few, if any, friends. Would it be possible for you to call on him next time you are at the hospital?" So the very next day my husband made his way out to General and stopped at Welti's bedside. I'll not forget the description he shared with me!

"I stepped into the ward," he said, "and found this little bewizened old man at the far end. What eyes, sharp and penetrating like headlights. And that large beak-like nose. He was a snuff user. A trickle of brown oozed from the corner of his mouth and stained the white sheet. A telltale sprinkle of the stuff was on the bedspread. He seemed glad when I introduced myself. And when I learned that he came from the German-speaking sector of Switzerland I tried the few phrases garnered from my school German on him. That really got through!

"First thing I knew he was pulling back the covers to show me the scars and lacings of his 14 operations. And when I shared some Bible verses and prayed with him, his eyes were moist. I'll never forget the grip of his hand as I left promising I'd come back soon!"

Well, that was the beginning of a beautiful chapter in our lives of the hundred-fold return of bread. When Emil was released from the hospital, he returned to his drab little room in a section of the city that had its own reputation. Here the rent was cheap, and as a bonus he had the companionship of cockroaches.

His release from the hospital came shortly before Christmas. This was a very special time for us—our first Christmas alone together as husband and wife. We had shared the previous Christmas festivities with both sides of the family. This was to be our first Christmas in the parsonage which was being bought by our monthly rental payment. Now our firstborn Jonathan would be two months old, and we were sure his bright eyes would love the lights on our tree and his ears would tune in to the singing of the carols. We were to be just us—our little family establishing our own tradition of blue lights on a simply decorated tree; of worshiping the manger child through Scripture, song, and prayers before giving any thought of the packages gathered under the pine branches. It was a beautiful anticipation!

Yet here we were, haunted as to the kind of Christmas Emil would have. In ignoring his need, wouldn't we be turning away the Christchild? We prayed about it and then Clarence went to hunt up Emil in his rooming house in the deteriorating section of downtown St. Paul. Clarence was to invite Emil to spend Christmas Eve and overnight with us so that he could be along at the early morning Christmas worship.

Clarence described his expedition when he returned that night. "I really was a bit frightened," he said, "no doubt about it since I was propositioned by more than one of these ladies as I made my way up to the third floor through those dimly lit corridors and up those creaky stairs. Locating his door number, I knocked loudly and kept on until I heard movement within. The door opened, and there Emil stood in his long union suit, so baggy at the knees that it looked for all the world as if he were ready to jump. His underwear served as pajamas at night as well as underclothes during the daytime. He bade me come in to his cheerless room.

"Emil," I began, "I've come to invite you to spend Christmas with us!" "Oh," was his response, "you got my letter then!"

"What letter?" I asked. "I wrote you," he continued, "about not knowing where I'd spend Christmas."

As Clarence told me this, I could only thank the Lord for making us unhappy about keeping Christmas all by ourselves. Even while Emil's letter was in the mails, God had put it on our hearts to send Clarence to invite him in person.

That next morning his letter came. Through all these years I've kept it with others he wrote to us:

Rev. Clarence T. Nelson,

Will you be so kind and answer my question if I could join your House of God in about three months from December 30, 1934. I belong to the Lutheran Church in Switzerland. Since I came in connection with you I find Jesus Christ and I wish I could stay with him until my time has come. Will you kindly see the members if they would accept me? I know Jesus Christ will and therefore I like to join your House of God. It is not too far for me to come because I love your sermon. I don't think I'm too much of a sinner. God bless you and your family as long as you live.

I will close my letter and hope you have a better Christmas than I have but I know God won't let me suffer.

The best thanks to you,
Emil Welti

P.S. If I can make the morning service I will gladly be there to enjoy a good service.

Please excuse my mistakes that I made in some of the words.

You can be sure we had a beautiful Christmas! And as long as he lived after that Emil spent every Christmas in our home.

It also came to be a regular thing for him to take Sunday dinner with us after church. Our family circle had been enlarged to include Lorraine and Walter Servheen. Both parents of these youth had died within a year of each other and God had guided us to open our home to them. An amazing thing was the beautiful friendship that developed between 17-year-old Wally and Emil. To Emil, Wally was the wonderful son he'd never had. To Wally, Emil was someone to love, someone who needed him. Lorraine became our beloved foster daughter, and Wally found a happy home with the Roligs who lived a block away. Our little house became too crowded after the next baby came to keep both these young folks. But Wally continued to have Sunday dinner with us. And so the friendship with Emil flourished. There was no prouder man in all the world when Wally gave Emil his last year's overcoat. Emil paraded it proud as a peacock. It was to him like a mantle of love enfolding him with warmth and protection from the cold world.

Earlier I mentioned that these were the depression times. Arlington Hill Church had been a tar-paper covered basement for 11 years. Big dreams of a roomy, fortress style church for this growing congregation had resulted in this first effort. Then it hit! That economic catastrophe with banks closing and long dole lines and veterans on the street corners selling apples and WPA and CCC Camps. In Arlington, 100 families were on relief. These were for the most part Scandinavian, skilled workers, for whom the door of employment had slammed shut. Church income withered accordingly. The congregation had paid no part of its benevolence apportionment for several years. And now they had been without a regular pastor for a year and a half. The dream of getting their sanctuary above ground seemed remote.

Emil was living on a welfare check of $30 a month. One Sunday after dinner he seemed disturbed about something. He was pacing up and down our living room. Suddenly he

20

turned to my husband and said, "It isn't right! It isn't right for God's house to be a basement like that. Your people wouldn't want to live in a basement home. Do you know what I'm going to do? This week I get my welfare check. I'm coming over with $10 to start that building fund!"

"But Emil," my husband protested, "I love your generosity! But that check is all you have for the whole month. You know how you live on bread and gravy through the week as it is. Why don't you wait until the end of the month and then see what money's left?" "No sir," was his response, "God will take care of me! This is what I'm going to do!"

And true to his word, on Wednesday of that week Emil came and presented a 10-dollar bill with which to begin the building fund. That started something! The next Sunday, in making announcements, Clarence gave this word to the congregation: "I hold in my hand a 10-dollar bill that tells a special story." Then he related what Emil had done, only he put it this way: "I don't want to embarrass him by naming him." At this point Emil proudly stood up there in the front row!

Well, it didn't happen over night, but in a short time things began to move. That 10-dollar bill primed the pump of people's giving and others got the idea of sharing out of their very necessities. So in spite of a plasterers' strike, and the conflict arising from the radical change in architecture, and our never knowing where the next payment was coming from, the walls and steel girders came to witness to the faith and spunk Emil's gift had sparked.

There's another facet having to do with shared bread returned manyfold in this sequence of events. My husband told his people he wouldn't lift his finger to raise one cent until the church first paid up their benevolence deficit. He felt there could be no blessing from God until we did this. So it was a proud heart, overflowing with gratitude, one day when he could present such a check to the conference. Then the bread began coming in for that upper structure.

And Emil? He lived to see that church dream fulfilled. He

moved over to our East Side, became a handyman in the bowling alley and mascot to the teams using those alleys. He had been accepted by that entire community and together with the church they all were his family.

When his frail body succumbed again to illness, my husband brought him to Bethesda Hospital, literally carrying that shrunken frame in his arms. In that first letter Emil had said, "I know Jesus Christ will accept me." And we know he did! Emil's memorial service was a beautiful tribute of how the Lord used a poor overlooked little man to work his plans for good. The funeral director donated his services. Even a grave was made available. The florist saw to it that Emil's casket had its blossoms. The bowling friends were out in numbers as was the congregation. He was anything but a pauper going to his final resting place "unsung and unknown." All witnessed to God's power in a man's life and gave praise to the Lord for the wonder of what one man's life can count for.

There is also this postscript. On one of the Christmases Emil spent with us, as we gathered around the tree after the usual worship, Clarence started to reach out for the gifts and to distribute them. Emil kept pointing to one particular package saying, "Take that one! Take that one!" Now Clarence had meant first to take some of the little gifts we had provided for Emil! But he honored Emil's request. And what do you think? Here was a present from Emil to the "Mrs."! Precious gift! Sure, it was a 10-cent glass candleholder from Woolworth's, but it might have been the finest crystal in the world as far as I was concerned. Emil knew I loved candlelight and he had provided me with a remembrance that has traveled with us wherever we have lived around the world. And still today we cherish it.

Bread—cast upon the waters!

A Cry for Love
Leads to a
Big Sister Movement

How often we miss what people's hearts are saying because we listen only to the words they use! This was our mistake with Judith Satterstrom. The enlightening and prodding of the Holy Spirit finally opened our ears.

She was a social worker for what was then known as The Lutheran Welfare Society. She appeared to be self-assured and independent, the soul of efficiency. We little dreamed, until later in our relationship, of the heart-hunger her self-assurance covered.

She sought us out because of a need she had in her work. "I have a real problem," she said. "Can you help me? Often I have to deal with delinquent girls, some of them expectant mothers. Many of them are alienated from their homes and need someone who will be a friend and love them. Aren't there young women in your congregation who would be willing to do this?" We invited her to our home for dinner so that we might probe this challenge with her.

When I think back to this encounter now, I remember the fuss she made over our children; how grateful she was for the simple dinner; how warm was her appreciation for everything. It was the beginning of a friendship and work together that provided many opportunities for her to break bread with us. Then we began to understand that her own deep need for love and understanding gave her a special sensitivity to this longing in others.

Orphaned as a little girl, she had set as her life's goal the service of helping lonely, needy girls. She had no known family. I remember how desperately she searched records, and followed the tiniest possible clues that might lead her to find her father, who had deserted her as a child. She wanted to show love to him. She wanted to know who she really was!

The Big Sister Movement of St. Paul's east side was born as a result of Judith's interest. We began by enlisting the young women in our church for this project. They, in turn, spread the word around to others until several churches were represented. Each would be assigned a young sister. Then Judith instructed the Big Sisters how they could be helpful. They were to meet their charges at least once a week. She emphasized the importance of gaining the confidence of the girl, not by forcing, but by loving acceptance of the girl as she was. Big Sisters were encouraged to make opportunities to have fun with their girls, to remember their birthdays, to do all the loving things a big sister would do for her own little sister.

It was a beautiful sight to see the double blessing of this experience. I remember getting ready for the Christmas dinner party at our house. At this time there were 20 youthful sisters. We pushed furniture against the walls and brought from church a long refectory table to expand the seating capacity of our dining table. Our little house on the hilltop corner of Burr and Magnolia had an open-end dining room, which permitted a table to extend into the living room. Everybody helped! Our children made favors and were a real part of the preparations. For the preceding weeks it was the subject of their prayers.

What laughter and singing filled our house that night! We thought it was lovely with candlelight and holly—and love. You couldn't miss it. It would be hard to say who was blessed the most: the young sisters who received beautiful gifts from their sponsors together with the knowledge that someone cared, or the big sisters who were so richly reaping the reward of the Lord's promise: "It is more blessed to give than to receive." This party was only the culmination of the friendships that were enriched and deepened week after week through the year.

Judith became a member of our church, and came to prize the family into which she had been received. I wonder how many Arlington Hill people today know the story of that clerestory window in the south side of the nave in their sanctuary. It was given anonymously at the time of building. The caption reads, "In gratitude from the stranger within your gates." That was Judith's gift. She had found her people in the family of God, and she had found fulfillment in providing a family for others.

The simple bread we broke came back a hundredfold.

When Cookies Are Bread

In the vocabulary of today's young people, bread has taken on quite different connotations from the one I knew as a youth. And yet, it still carries with it the implication of provision. We often use "dough" in the same way. That was our synonym for money. I have an idea that the "bread" the Lord spoke of in his promise wasn't confined to one pattern or form. I think it could well include our cookie project.

Clarence and I wanted our children to learn that Christmas was a time for giving, a time for remembering people because we were remembering the One whose birthday it was. This wasn't hard for them to understand. They received gifts on their birthdays. Shouldn't he receive them on his?

So we conceived the idea of making a list of old people in our church who might find it difficult to bake cookies. It was quite a list, and when Clarence found that, for free, he could get metal cans that had been used for film reels, he decided they were just the thing. It never occurred to him to ascertain how many cookies it would take to fill each can. They were huge!

He enlisted the children's help in painting them; some blue, some green. Then Clarence would paint a star, or a candle, or a pine tree, or an angel on the cover. They really were attractive. Mine was the job to provide the filler.

Now when I think of all those cookies rolling out of our oven, I get weary. But when you are young, and love what you are doing, it's fun. Icebox cookies, Christmas tree cookies, ginger cookies, raisin cookies, and Swedish sprits and pinnar sticks, and chocolate oatmeal cookies—there was no end to it! I commandeered every container in the house to protect them from the little human mice that found them tempting.

At last, with paper lace doilies lining them, the cans were filled and ready, and we had our list in hand. Our plan was to have the children join us after school so that together we could sing carols for the folks. And just seeing the little ones was a real therapy for the aged. However, because of the long list, we decided to get an early start. We discussed whether we should begin at the far end of our list, or closer to home. We were led to the latter, and chose to make the first call on the mother of our organist. Helen was not only a gifted organist, but a beautiful vocalist as well. Her mother was a widow living in an upper duplex, less than a mile from our home.

How I wish everyone could know the wonder of the Holy Spirit's leading! Surely he must have nudged us to go to Mrs. Johnson's first! As we knocked on the outer door, the landlady came out, worry and concern written on her face. "I'm so glad somebody has come," she said. "I've heard no sound from upstairs since late last night and I keep wondering if Mrs. Johnson is all right." Fortunately, she had a key to the upper apartment, so she could let us in, when there was no response to our knock.

What a sight greeted our eyes as we entered! Apparently this dear mother had been stricken with a heart attack and had tried to get to the bathroom. She hadn't made it, and there she lay on the floor in the midst of a mess completely opposite to her Scandinavian sense of cleanliness. At a glance we knew that her spirit had departed to be with the Lord. My husband set about to call the doctor and an ambulance and her family. We didn't dare to touch her until the doctor arrived, but I

27

was able to clean up the mess on the floor before her children came. Their gratitude for that, and that we should have been the ones to find her, was a beautiful reward.

There was an in-depth flavor to the succeeding calls. The meaning of Christmas—Immanuel—God with us—became very clear. We learned anew what it meant through faith in the Christ of Bethlehem and Golgotha, to be able to say, "Whether I live or die, I am the Lord's."

Who can calculate what the returns of our Christmas cookie project were in the lives of those who received and those who gave!

Bread on a Bed

How amazing it is to find that when you think you're doing something for someone else, you receive far more than you give. Isn't this a case of serendipity? My Saturday nights at the bedside of Cliff Boren were like that.

We ran a busy household with four little ones to provide for and an open door of hospitality. These were the depression years so we did not have means to hire help. They were the days before "wash and wear" garments had been discovered, so many times I'd find myself ironing late at night. It seemed to be the only time left to get to the bottom of the basket. The bundle of unmended stockings got carted to any of the meetings where my fingers shuttled that darning needle weaving the patch across each hole. But Saturday night was my night after the children had been bathed and snugged in bed. Clarence was in his study reviewing his sermon for the morrow, and I was free to leave the house. That's how I came to read poetry to our young pastor friend.

It was through an earlier experience when he rode with us to Rock Island that we had discovered his affinity for poetry. How quickly the miles flew by as we each shared our favorites. I loved Richard Burton's poem:

When I am overmatched with petty cares
    And things of earth loom large and seem to be
      of moment,
How it soothes and comforts me
    To step into the night and feel the airs of heav-
      en fan my cheek
Such things as these make earthly cares seem light
    and temporal.

He matched this with Gray's "Elegy in a Country Church Yard":

The curfew tolls the knell of parting day,
    The lowing herd winds slowly o'er the lea.
The plowman homeward plods his weary way
    And leaves the world to darkness and to me.

That is how I had come to read poetry to our young pastor friend, so crippled beyond what seemed humanly possible to bear.

But first let me tell you about Cliff Boren as a handsome athletic young man at college. He cut quite a figure and was flavoring the joy of being alive. Then a teacher presented a challenge to Cliff and he decided to enter the ministry. Even his parents tried to dissuade him at that time, for they thought he had all too many gifts to be "wasted" in the ministry. But Cliff's commitment was very real and he persisted until he had completed the seminary and was ordained. He then was assigned to a three-point parish in the iron range and also what was the vestibule to Minnesota's beautiful lake region: Deerwood, Ironton, and Crosby.

He loved his parishes, and gave himself wholeheartedly to shepherding these people. Then gradually at first, but each year worsening, arthritis crept its insidious way through his body. Soon its crippling effects were for all to see. It didn't help his perspective any to acknowledge his mother's disability from the same disease.

Every possible medical resource was explored but to no avail. Finally he had to give up his beloved pastorate. He was then brought to Bethesda Hospital in St. Paul. Cliff's body was broken, but not his spirit. There was that day when he lifted his coverings to show us his twisted feet. We who were healthy had no way of knowing what pains and torment attended this process. The nurses of Bethesda would tell us how they would roll out his bed into a corridor on a Sabbath morning and from this strange pulpit he would give the sermon. Many witnessed to the power of these life-changing messages.

When the hospital staff concluded that they had done all they could for him, he was brought to his parental home by ambulance. Since it was on the East Side close to my husband's church it was natural that Clarence became his pastor. It was his habit to drop in on Cliff several times each week to share prayer and readings from Scripture. What a privilege this was for us all!

Coming back then to my Saturday nights. Former English teacher that I was, I loved poetry. It was a delight to read my favorite poems to Cliff since he loved this form of literary expression too. One special time was unforgettable! I had read Milton's sonnet on his blindness and we discussed the different implications of that last line, "He also serves who only stands and waits!" During the week I had come across a little contemporary gem that I thought applied to Cliff.

> A crystal mirror I,
>   fate flung me, how prosaic,
>   In the dust.
>   Now shattered here I lie!
> Lord, help me to try
>   to be a rare mosaic
> In the dust.

Cliff loved it, and mused on his own situation in the light of these lines. So he began creating. From time to time he would show me things he had dictated to those serving him. By now his hands had become so crippled that he couldn't hold a pen. His whole body was wracked with pain. In his last year he became totally blind.

But what a ministry went out from that bedside! People came to him to warm themselves at the fires of his faith. He had a running correspondence with that great soul, George Washington Carver, who had discovered that oil from peanuts had therapeutic value even for arthritis.

He began collecting crosses. They came from many parts of the world. Through this correspondence he was able to witness to the power of the cross of Christ in his own life. His favorite one was a crucifix with a varnished background made up of innumerable half-burned matches. This one seemed to be a parable of his own life; a match lighted—only to flare up and then be blown out before it seemingly had begun to be used. Yet what a radiant background these half-burned matches made for the cross of Christ. And do you wonder that when he came to preaching Cliff's funeral my husband carried this into the pulpit to hold high?

For Cliff this wasn't just a hobby. His desire was that these crosses should offer the opportunity to tell the old, old story of Jesus and his love.

The next Saturday evening after the one when we had read Milton's sonnet, Cliff showed me his offering along the same line of thought. He entitled it:

GETHSEMANE

Gethsemane is mine—
For I have walked with him there.
I breathed a prayer tonight
That was so hard to pray
I hardly dared to utter it.
But I am not afraid,
For my Savior knows my heart.
I prayed that if I served
Him best right here upon my bed,
That he could keep me here.
Then I prayed for strength

32

That I might be content,
And within me understand—
That only he serves well
Who knows no time or place!

Clarence had some beautiful experiences those days when the reality of heaven came closer and closer. One night, out of his physical blindness, Cliff broke forth with a sudden expression of joy, "I see! Oh, I see! It's beautiful. It's beautiful." And another time it was as if the windows of heaven had opened. He exclaimed, "The trees! The green trees! The beautiful trees!" Once when they were discussing prayer, Cliff admitted that sometimes he pushed past mere words. "I'm just like that big shepherd dog I once owned. The position he loved best was to lie at my feet and look up at me with those liquid hazel eyes. I too can lie at Jesus' feet just looking up and adoring and forget all about the passing of time."

After hovering in the gray haze of the border country for several days he said to my husband at his bedside, "I'm in the shadows now, but a call is sounding, bidding me to come into the sunshine!"

Cliff's favorite Scripture was Psalm 27, and he meditated on the promise it holds out that he would soon be going to the "land of the living." Before his final tap on the shoulder, he planned every detail of his memorial service: one to be at Arlington Hills Church, and another at the Ironton, Deerwood, Crosby Parish. He requested that Dr. Glenn Clark give his obituary. Dr. Clark had been a frequent visitor at Cliff's bedside and had enlisted his army of "fanner bees," as he was wont to call his band of intercessors, to lift Cliff up to God for healing. And soon now Cliff was to know perfect healing. He also dictated to Clarence what became his last will and testament and asked that the family be assembled after the funeral for the reading of the same. In it he conferred upon them each for his own accepting the priceless inheritance of Christ as Savior.

It was quite an experience to carry out these wishes! It became a spiritual enrichment that has been a benediction on each of us involved and one that doesn't wear thin with the passing of years.

What a nourishing loaf of bread came from that bed!

Around the World
with a Waffle

Surely waffles are a form of bread, and what a variety one finds around the world. It's not without meaning that in the story of the temptation of our Lord the devil took a stone in hand saying, "If you are the Son of God command this stone to become bread . . . " Those worn and flattened stones were the very shape of the bread common to that day. Well do Clarence and I recall the wide flattened biscuit of the Arabs. And when we lived in Switzerland we loved the fragrant "flute bread" fresh from the oven. It was a common sight to see a lad pass by with two or three of these unwrapped loaves tucked under his arm.

My husband's pastorate in Duluth was during the war years 1940-46. An important part of his ministry was to keep close contact with the service personnel on the widely scattered fronts of that war. He made it his goal to have a personalized letter in the mails each month, and there were more than 125 of them. When home on furlough the servicemen were guests in our home for lunch. Because I knew waffles weren't the ordinary fare in the armed services, I made this the bill of fare. We served a variety of them. One of their specials was apple-cinnamon. And because we were close to blueberry country, we had our own blueberry jam and syrup. When possible we would also have little pigs or crisp bacon, that is when coupons could be saved for this purpose. Some of our single friends who ate out a great deal, made it a point to slip us their unused coupons. Needless to add, the young men were delighted and ate with zest.

But the food was the least important of these experiences. We really traveled around the world at our table as these young men (I don't remember any girls in the service then) related their experiences. There was Bob who was stationed in the Aleutians. In later years, as we conducted retreats to the families of the Armed Forces in Alaska, we were privileged to be on the Aleutians, and there we understood the isolation Bob had described. This isolation made the men want to climb the walls. These feelings were brought on by the low-roofed Quonset huts, the endless buffeting of the winds, and the leaden skies. And if by rare chance the sun came out it would be only for a scant three hours at the most in winter. And besides there was that treeless, weed-strewn hump of an island whichever way one looked. Small wonder that many were sent home with unstrung nerves and that Bob harbored a real fear that he too could join them. A glance at our children who shared all this made one realize the deep effect these conversations had on them. Rarely a night went by but what they remembered Bob in their prayers.

Then there was "Chuck," the marine from Okinawa. As he savored the waffles, he told us what it was like to be in the jungle without food. They had bailed out of their crippled plane and landed in a jungle thicket. Surrounded by enemies they dared not give away their hiding place. Hungry as they were, they knew that climbing a tree to retrieve the food-drop their buddies had released would be fatal. And all the while they were slowly dying of hunger! Between clenched teeth, he muttered, "I tell you dead, uncooked crow comes to taste good at that point!" He never did return from his next assignment.

Then there was Harold of the Air Force. He loved flying.

"It was as if we could reach out our hands and touch the face of God as one soared above the clouds. How inconsequential so many of one's earthly concerns seemed up there," he would say. He hated worse than sin the dropping of those bombs and shuddered as he shared the haunting awareness of the destruction those block busters would wreak. And Harold didn't come back either (14 gold stars shone in their field of blue on the church's service flag hanging in the narthex). In his next to the last mission before he was due to return, his plane was downed by flak. What comfort his widowed mother drew from our retelling Harold's witness at our table when he quietly said, "Whether I live, or whether I die, I am the Lord's!"

When at long last the bundle of Harold's personal effects reached his mother's cottage the most memorable among them was his well-marked Bible. Psalm 139 was heavily underscored: "if I take the wings of the morning, and dwell in the uttermost parts of the sea, even there thy hand shall lead me and thy right hand shall hold me." Written clearly in the margin was the date of Harold's last flight!

The stack of waffles was finally put by and the last cup of our Swedish brew of coffee was downed as these experiences were being shared. Then came the real climax of the visit, a season of prayer together. These young men became a part of our larger family.

Do you wonder that down the years, many, many times we have received words of appreciation and the witness to what it had all meant to them. How privileged we have been to be whisked around the world on the magic carpet of a waffle.

How Edna's Loaves Multiplied

The heart of a very dear friend had been really touched by the Lord. She was our children's Sunday school teacher in Duluth. Her concern was that her income was so meager that she had very little to give. But the Lord touched her imagination with his finger and she found a novel way to supplement her giving.

As a clerk in a women's dress shop Edna's salary was modest. Moreover, she was the support of her aged widowed mother. Clarence and I learned to know Edna in a special way following that bitter cold New Year's night when her blessed mother was struck by a bus as she waited on the corner. In our concern we visited her at the hospital and there developed a beautiful personal relationship. And that is how we learned about her bread-baking project for the Lord.

Duluth has a large Scandinavian population, and home-made Swedish rye bread was really prized. So what did Edna do? One day each week on coming home from work she set a big dough with rye flour and butter and other good things. Then while she busied herself with her supper the bread was left to rise. And late before retiring she would proceed to bake these neatly formed loaves. In the morning she tucked all those crusty nut brown loaves into a huge basket and caught her bus for the store. Fellow workers eagerly snapped up as much as she could carry. But Edna never deducted one cent for the flour and the rest of the ingredients. She dedicated all of it to some special project for her Lord. What she gave from this source was over and above her usual tithe.

Edna tells the story of a friend who asked her to make some home-baked fruit cake before Christmas. She did that over the next weekend and when her friend paid Edna she said, "The contents of this cake are really costly. Surely you should deduct the costs and give the rest. But our Edna kept back only one dollar which anyone would know wouldn't begin to cover the fruit and nuts that go into a rich fruit cake. The following story is about that dollar she held out. And when Edna tells it she always concludes, "That was the time I think I heard God laugh."

Here is that story. The following Sunday Edna was in church as usual. She had with her the tithe for the offering plus a special check covering the proceeds from the fruit cake. How was she to know that a special feature of that service was a presentation by a member of the Gideon Bible Society. He concluded by calling for a special offering at the door for Bibles to place in hotels and motels. Out came that dollar bill she had tucked away in her purse. And as she put it on the plate held in the hand of that Gideon Bible Society speaker she said she thought she heard God chuckle over her shoulder.

Now where did Edna's bread get cast? Our children can tell you about that. Biz, our daughter in Indonesia whom Edna had taught in Sunday school, was a regular correspondent. And through Biz Edna learned of a young Indonesian who would have to quit school in mid semester because of his father's untimely death. There just were no funds to cover. Edna accepted him as her ward and literally put him through the medical school with her rye bread dollars. Isn't this "bread upon the waters"?

David our son is pastor of a black church in a Chicago

ghetto. Edna has made his Bethel Church one of her prayer projects. Glowingly David writes about those amazing checks from Edna which come like manna from the skies always at a time of crisis. This money goes to Christian Action Ministry, or to the Academy for dropouts, a joint effort of 12 churches working to bring hope to many, to a sheltered workshop for the physically deprived, and to the several day care centers for the children of working mothers. This endeavor carries the name, "Ash Flower Operation" since it began in the wake of those ghetto riots a few years ago and the accompanying holocaust.

Edna eventually left off clerking and became a practical nurse as a better way to help people at the time of their need. For many years she lovingly served in the Deaconess Home in Omaha, working with the aged. Lengthening years and failing strength made retirement necessary. However don't think she folded her hands and took to a rocking chair. Not our Edna. She is even now a volunteer giving her services to the elderly. Yes, and she still bakes bread and sends off those checks. Her only regret is that she can't do more.

But God's promise states that what we do will return to us. How does it then get back to Edna? Each summer she makes her pilgrimage to our log cabin at Moose Lake, Minnesota. This is her way of renewing a dear friendship. And one look at her lovely face and you know that beauty is more than skin deep. Her inner joy and peace and trust is written indelibly on her face.

Strangers Are Brothers

The war of the '40s and some of the inhuman accompaniments were a great concern to us. We were aroused about the injustice the nisei, our Japanese-American citizens, had to go through after Pearl Harbor. They were herded into concentration camps and dispossessed of their homes and holdings. What a distorted perspective war can bring about! How utterly inhuman we can become! We lump everybody in one group and condemn them all. It is to be remembered in this connection that not one single instance of sabotage was ever uncovered.

For the most part these artistic people from a distant shore had become very good citizens. Their eye for beauty and orderliness was evidenced in the way they displayed the lush California fruits and vegetables. Their industry was attested to in their quickly becoming able to sustain themselves. Yet in the blindness of war we forget that all men are brothers, and we categorize and condemn, without any sense or personal justice. This story is one about how strangers became brothers.

Through the Council of Churches we learned about some of the young men in this predicament. They could be released to fill needed jobs if these opened up. At this time, the bean sprout industry was being launched in Duluth. Of course they had to have sponsors and were kept under surveillance. We agreed to sponsor three of them.

We've never had finer young men in our home. We thought it was an invaluable experience for our growing, impressionable children. We have seen the fruit of these experiences many times in their lives.

When they came to us, it was Christmas time, and they were made a part of the family. They were to stay with us until we could find housing for them and their work would begin. What fun the family had in shopping for their Christmas presents! Duluth was cold compared with California, so warm scarves and fur-lined gloves were a welcome addition to their wardrobes.

It was interesting to watch the children at "tree-time" that Christmas Eve! First, there was the reading of the incomparable Christmas story, with each member of the family taking a portion. How attentive our guests were! And they joined us in singing the carols as best they could. It wasn't hard to recall the scene on the Judean hills that first Christmas when the angel chorus burst out from the heavens to startle the humble shepherds keeping watch over their flock by night. In the prayers that followed, our children participated, as was our custom, and it was moving to hear the childlike petitions on behalf of these new friends. They prayed for their families from whom they were separated; they prayed for their work and their housing; and they thanked God that they had come to us.

Then came gift distribution time. Which packages do you think Jon, Dave, Biz, and Mary pointed to with eager fingers as the first to be distributed? It wasn't those with their names. It was those they had wrapped for their new friends! And the veracity of Scripture, "It is more blessed to give than to receive," was never more clearly demonstrated. I cannot describe for you the joy shining on those faces as they watched their friends pull away the wrappings to open their gifts.

These new friends went Christmas caroling with us to the

shut-ins; they shared with us in the hospitality of our church people; they became like brothers in our family.

It wasn't very long before their work was found and some light housekeeping rooms secured. Even then they would join us for happy family times. Come spring and we would picnic on the rocky shores of Gitche Gumee. The children would share something of America's origin as they told of the beautiful Indian people to whom this land first belonged. (They omitted that part of our history of which some of us are so ashamed—the part of how we got the land!) We would watch the sun go down and sit in quiet meditation worshiping. Our friends revelled in the bountiful beauty of the north country.

We were ambivalent in our feelings, after the war had ceased, when we learned they could return to their homes in California. We rejoiced with them that their confinement was over; but we hated to have these new friends leave. They had truly become like our brothers.

Surely it must be experiences like this that have made each of our children sensitive to human injustice, and very ready to champion the cause of the oppressed. If you read their life stories, you will see this bread compounded and reenergized beyond anything one could dream.

The Amazing
Geography of Bread

British Guiana? Where was that? This was the question our children asked when we told them we were to have house guests from this far country. So we sought out a globe, pointing out the country our guests hailed from and decided it was a long way from Duluth. Moreover, we knew next to nothing about it, so even before our guests arrived, we were already learning.

Pastor and Mrs. Magalee were charming people. India was the place of their birth, but by fortuitous circumstance, they had come to live in British Guiana. Pastor Magalee told us how as a little boy he had been left an orphan with the street as his home. Here he was picked up by a missionary who reared him as his own son and made possible educational opportunities for him. As he matured into manhood, he decided he wanted to be a missionary like his foster father for he knew that it was the love of Christ constraining this father that had prompted him to open his home to a homeless lad. And so Hector became Pastor Magalee.

Then there came the opening in British Guiana. The church had decided to serve this new field and a pastor was needed. The call came to Pastor Magalee and it was from this his adopted country where he had spent most of his adult years, he now came to the United States to spread the word of how God was at work in British Guiana.

What a privilege was ours to have them as our guests! They were bright, gentle, loving people who entranced our children by the stories they told.

When the boys were telling them about our fishing at Sand Lake where we had our "Koja" Pastor Magalee asked, "What do you use for bait?" One of our boys said, angleworms, the other, minnows. Then Biz piped up to say, "Sometimes we use little wooden minnows with hooks!" Mary was too little to know much about it. Then our new British Guiana friend said, "Let me tell you how we fish in our country. There are many fish in our fast moving mountain streams and they're an important source of food for our people. But there is a special way to catch them. The fishermen make little balls out of a combination of herbs. The formula is a family secret and is only shared from father to son. They'll give you some balls to fish with but they won't tell you how they make the balls."

"Like for us not telling where a specially good fishing hole is," piped up Jon. "Well, something like that," said Dr. Magalee, "but not quite. As I said they will give you balls with which to fish, but they feel if they gave the secret of them away, they wouldn't be able to get enough fish for their families."

"How do they fish with those balls?" Biz wanted to know.

Dr. Magalee laughed, "It really is funny," he said. "You see they don't use hooks at all. They throw the balls (which are quite small) into the stream, and immediately they begin to sink. As they do, the fish come and nibble on them. Whatever there is in these balls, we don't know, but when a fish has nibbled enough he becomes sort of drunk and he jumps out of the water again and again. This is when the fishermen spear him. It's quite a sport!"

Later that week we heard our children regaling their playmates with the story of this amazing way of fishing.

Another true story he told left our children wide-eyed and

thoughtful. He was telling about a certain tribe that had the strange belief that anything you dreamed should be acted out at once. One of the children giggled at that and just couldn't be contained. When I asked him why, he said he dreamed he was out playing in the street without a stitch of clothing on! Dr. Magalee grinned but went on to say that children went to bed full of fears, because they never knew when they might be awakened in the middle of the night and hauled out of their beds because their father had dreamed they should be living in another place.

Then he told how that in these same homes children would often go to bed hungry because their family meal would be served up in a big wooden bowl, and the father always helped himself first. Usually he took such a big helping that there wasn't enough to go around. "That wasn't very nice!" was Biz's interpolation. "No, it wasn't," our friend replied, "but the father had never been taught any other way! Maybe you'd like to know about the dishes on which they ate their food. Before the meal, the mother would send the children to the pond to gather lily pads. These they brought home, and then became their dinner plates!" "That would make easy dishwashing," observed Dave. "All you would have to do would be to throw them back in the pond."

"Exactly," said Dr. Magalee. "But now I'd like to tell you about the change I saw in a home like that. One day a man came to tell that father about an almighty heavenly Father, how he loved us all, and how he sent his Son Jesus to be our Savior. There were many times of talking together and then the man brought a 'talking book' and taught the father to read it."

"I'll bet that was the Bible," was Biz's offering.

"You're right," our friend responded. "And the most beautiful thing of all is that as that father read about Jesus, and how he fed them when they were hungry, and even took little children in his arms to love them—well, something happened to that father. He wanted to be like Jesus."

Then Dr. Magalee described the change that took place in

46

that home. He told of how at mealtime the father now served the others first, and saw to it that food was divided so that everybody had some. And before bedtime, the father would gather the children around him and read them stories from the big book. Then they would fall asleep secure in the knowledge that their heavenly Father kept watch over them. What a change, surely as radical as when St. Paul was spun around on the Damascus Road.

In the evening of Dr. Magalee's stay we were dinner guests of Dr. Tilderquist and his sister Eva. They were deeply interested in the spread of the gospel. The doctor, an eye, ear, nose specialist, was fascinated to hear Dr. Magalee tell of a potion the aborigines smeared on their arrows when game hunting at a distance from their village. This too was a secret. When an animal was pierced by such an arrow he would go into a coma instead of dying. This meant the hunters could carry the inert creature so anesthetized the long distance through the tropical heat with no danger of the meat spoiling. The doctor reported afterwards that he learned that this native secret had been ferreted out with success and that New York surgeons were using it in the most delicate of operations. These ancients had furnished modern medical technology with a compound that made possible the freezing of an area for the most delicate kinds of surgery.

To stop and marvel at the geography of bread is to realize all afresh that he who said, "I am the bread of the world," meant it not only for British Guiana but for everyone in every land. Our children around our table had an unforgettable lesson in world geography, one they learned not from a book but from real people.

God Hasn't
Given Up on You, Peg!

Our Washington ministry was heavily slanted towards alcoholics by the very fact that this proud capital city consumes more alcoholic beverages than any other American city. The social drinking in high places and the pressures to conform go with life in Washington. Many of these "sick" people came to live in the shabby run-down housing to be found in the environs of our Augustana Church. They "holed" themselves up in these cheap rooms seeking to drown their wretchedness as the flame of their lives burned low. More than one knocked at Augustana's door for help. And with the active visitation to every address in what we called "Operation One Mile" we came to know their desperate need and reached out to help.

I began a regular Bible class at Occuquan, the reformatory for women located in Virginia on the outer fringe of the metropolis. I continued this weekly class for seven years. The chaplain of the Lutheran Welfare Society often requested me to minister to the needs of individual women.

On one of those first visits the chaplain asked if I would visit Margaret Dunbar in her cell. He'd had a long counseling session with her that day. He said, "She wants out of our world and says suicide is her only answer." This is how I met Margaret who was to become a part of our lives. Peg's dossier showed more than 100 sentences for alcoholism. She had become a notorious case in police files. Her chemical dependence had beaten her to the ground and Peg wanted to throw in the sponge in her battle with an enemy whose power to destroy grew with every defeat. "What's the use?" she told me. "My sentence is soon up. And what'll happen? The district will put 50 cents in my pocket and then bus me and the others being released to the district line. And who do you suppose will be there to meet us and celebrate the prison doors having closed behind us and our being set free? All those old drinking pals, the old goats who'll set right to work to pull us down into the gutter once again. What other alternative is open to me needing a roof over head and daily food? And so the whole ugly cycle begins all over again. Do you wonder, Mrs. Nelson, that for me death is the only way out?"

I realized that this poor woman with her willpower all but shattered by drink, needed something more than a Bible verse. She needed prayers that had legs! I spoke up, "Peg, I'll tell you what. I'll personally meet the bus. You are to come home to us as you make a fresh start. We'll do everything within our power to get you on your feet. Let's kneel together right now in this cell while you turn your life over into God's time!"

And so it was that we met the reformatory bus with its sad lot of women. It was as Peg had described. There was the tag-end company of red-faced men whose way of life was written plain on face and clothing, the welcoming committee to insure there would be another whirl on the merry-go-round that once again would fling these women into the wretched pool of misery at Occuquan.

Once under our roof, Peg walked as in a dream. "God is here," she kept repeating. "He sent you into my life, that I know. I've done nothing to deserve this!" In those ensuing days she told the tragic story of her life. God had put in her hand gifts of intelligence and personality which as a secretary won for her one promotion after another. Indeed she had become circulation manager for Vanity Fair, a top-notch woman's magazine. Her work took her across the country and even abroad. But the job was a pressure cooker, and for a time liquor was the easy way out. Then it became her master and soon she was out in the street, her clothing and belongings pawned, one by one, as she became the consort of one or the other alcoholic men who drew her to their side. No wonder she had that lengthened record of commitments to the reformatory! Her family had come to her rescue again and again in the early stages, but now they had given up and pulled their hands off. We sought to put the stars back in her sky by an oft-repeated theme, "But God hasn't given up on you, Peg!"

So we set about to arrange for eyeglasses and wardrobe. The help of folks in our congregation made the job easy. Clothes and gifts of money seemed to come "right out of the woodwork." Landing a job was quite a bit tougher. Here Dr. Robert Van Deusen, public relations director for the National Lutheran Council and a personal friend, was a great help. Learning through us of Peg's background in the magazine field he wondered if her talents might not be used in the publication of a monthly Lutheran Servicemen's publication issued in one of the offices in the headquarters building just a block from our Augustana Church.

Soon she was pecking away at a typewriter, and beyond that showing her editorial skills when deadlines called for every hand to help. Soon she was doing more and more of the editorial job, winning many a kudo from those in charge. So with her first check we set her up in light housekeeping rooms in the vicinity of her work. However, again and again she'd be at our home for meals. We knew all too well the devil's use of loneliness. Sunday worship services at Augustana became an anchorage and her sparkling personality and warmth of spirit won her a ready-made family. Those people literally threw their arms about her.

Clarence and I took Peg with us on our monthly turn to lead services at Union Gospel Mission downtown. Peg felt right at home in this setting of broken-down transients. Testimonials were always invited after the sermon. In an instant, Peg was on her feet to witness that she too had been plucked like a brand from its burning. In a powerful way she quoted Psalm 40: "He drew me up from the desolate pit, out of the miry bog. And set my feet upon a rock," adding, "This is my story. I've found that rock which is Christ. I have my feet on that solid foundation. Praise the Lord!"

Peg made her regular attendance at the nearby Alcoholics Anonymous chapter a religious duty. But in this connection we made the unhappy discovery that some who were less committed came to AA meetings to single out a faltering one to lure to their bedrooms. My eyes were opened. I knew the church ought to take this activity under its wings, too. Soon we opened an AA meeting at Augustana. Clarence tried to be there at each of those meetings and to make himself available as a spiritual counselor.

"Do you know what?" Peg would say to us again and again during those months when she was happily at work, "God is always right there by my typewriter." We believed that she was finally free because she evidently was walking hand in hand with her Lord those many weeks. Her happy disposition and ebullient spirits made her fun to be with.

Then one day, like a bolt out of the blue, the devil reached from behind and cut her down. Taverns were on every side in that area, and one day on passing an open tavern door, and hearing the old familiar noises, she was lured in "for just one drink," and that's all it took. Great was the fall of a woman who had come a long way toward personal redemption. Just by chance Clarence drove down the street where she had fallen. She was being helped to her feet by one of Augustana's members, a retired practical nurse. She also had chanced by. Then occurred a sight that must have made the angels sing. Minnie Thompson was embracing and kissing her and offering her strong arm to tottering Peg.

Once again we took her to our home hoping to dry her out and have her back at her work. But have you ever tried tc "dry out" an alcoholic? Sneaky and clever beyond all imagination, they will find some way to break out and fetch that next drink. So it happened that while Clarence was at home guarding Peg from herself, an emergency call demanded that he hurry to the hospital. Clarence hid Peg's clothes and outer coat in a dark corner of the basement on the pipes above the oil tank. She'd never think to look there. When Clarence returned, Peg was gone.

After a few days she telephoned. Her slurred words and loud talk gave her away. She'd engaged a room in a nearby hotel. Enlisting the help of Dr. Van Deusen, we found her and persuaded her to come with us in the car. Drunk and cursing, she was loaded into our car and we were off for home. Peg was literally "demon-possessed" at such times. A strange inversion of her whole being took place. On arriving at the parsonage we had a problem. Peg refused to budge from the car. Finally Clarence called me to see if I could persuade her. When gentle pleading proved of no avail, I said sternly, "Well, Peg, we have no other choice. Apparently you want me to call the police who'll take you back to Occuquan. The other alternative is to come in and let me give you a hot bath and some coffee!" Her leering, drunken response was, "OK then. And I suppose these two preachers will help me with the bath, ha! ha!" This was all too much for Bob Van Deusen who broke out in a burst of laughter, good medicine for all of us. So Clarence and Bob pulled Peg from the car, and with one preacher under either arm they walked her up the stairs. In minutes I had her soaking in the tub and soon after had tucked her in the covers.

This is not the end of Peg's tale. There were other "ups and downs," times when we had to "truck" her out to the district hospital to be dried out. It was law that such needy souls could not be forced against their will to take this treatment. So on one of these times Peg stubbornly refused to sign in even though we had spent more than an hour with her in the emergency room waiting our turn. Finally the busy nurse said, "Look, I'll help another patient for the moment while you two talk this out." Our persuasion wasn't enough to counteract the devil who held Peg in his power. Finally in desperation Clarence took Peg's hand and scrawled her signature. No one could say it wasn't her handwriting. So we thought, but when the nurse returned and asked, "Miss Dunbar, is this your signature?" Peg's answer was, "Lordy, no; the preacher forced my hand." That time we did what AA advises. "There comes the time when your only option is to pull your hand away and let them go!" Our last glimpse of Peg Dunbar was watching her reel down the sidewalk on her way to another Occuquan cycle.

Remembering our Lord's word, "I was in prison and you visited me," Clarence visited Occuquan to sit with Peg and bring her God's Word and to pray with her. We would not give up on Peg. So when this term was over she was back with us at the parsonage. This time as we paid the advance rental she insisted on some reimbursement. Now her last job had been with a realty firm offering Washingtonians Florida lots. And Peg had been persuaded to make some monthly payments on one as investment. She had made five payments of $10 each and her proposition was to turn this over to us. Those five monthly payments had been the measure of that last stretch of sobriety. But once again she tumbled and once again we picked her up to help her try again. This time it was to share a room with another unhappy soul, Clara Toller, who we were trying to dry out. The two of them were using the room of our two daughters who were away at school. When Peg complained of pain around the heart, we arranged a doctor's appointment and that afternoon drove her to his office. When I offered to pick her up, Peg who was well aware of my crowded schedule refused the lift. She said, "Now Ruth, you know what it's like to wait your turn. I'll just not have you waiting for me. I'll call a cab, Ruth, don't you fear."

Peg never did make it home. The doctor's word must have been upsetting and it was more than she could face. Late that afternoon the telephone rang in Clarence's office. By the background noises and raucus laughter and by Peg's own scrambled words, he knew that she was at a tavern telephone. Clarence wormed out of her the address and told her to be looking. In minutes he was at the curb, and leaving the car running, managed to coax her to come home. Once home we sat with her before the fireplace trying to put together what had happened. But a person "in the cups" just doesn't make too much sense. She did say, "Nelsons, I am a big sinner. But I also know that I'm a sinner saved by grace. Didn't Jesus say: 'No one shall pluck them out of my hands'"? Later we helped her upstairs to her bed. Presently she was calling for Clarence to come up. She was in the bathroom standing before the mirror. "Pastor, do you want to see a death-head?" all the while pointing to her face reflected in the mirror. It was pasty and all but drained of its blood. It was clear then that the doctor must have indicated that her days were running out and that the old pump was about to give up. Again it was more than she could face.

That next morning I came to her room, and after I recovered from the shock I called Clarence. "Hurry home, Clarence. Peg is dead in her bed!" Then I told him how I had come with a breakfast tray and looked on Peg's inert and expressionless face. Peg had gone to claim the mercy of the Savior she had so clearly confessed.

Well, we summoned Peg's family from New York. That fine sister and her husband never did get through expressing gratitude that Peg could slip away in the peace and shelter of our home. In looking through her purse, they came across a little prayer dated from the first time Peg had talked with me in her cell: "Thank you, God, for putting a Good Samaritan across my path." The four pastors who had had part in her rescue, carried her casket from the church to the grave. We were amazed, moreover, at the many who attended that service celebrating Peg's relinquishment of the cross and her laying hold of heaven's never fading crown.

God never gives up on any of us, and he hadn't given up on Peg.

Agneta Takes Bread to Sweden

She was a winsome lass with her golden hair, her sky-blue eyes, and her rosy outdoor complexion. You hardly had to hear her speak to know she was an example of the finest womanhood that old Sweden produced.

She came to our church in Washington seeking fellowship with other youth of her age. Her parents had permitted her at the tender age of 17 to travel to America to perfect her English as well as to gather experience from a year of living in a foreign country. She had secured employment as a maid and nursemaid in a suburban home and found herself desperately isolated and lonely. On her day off she sought out a church of Scandinavian background. She found more than a church. She found a home, and our lives were enriched by another "daughter."

The pattern of American church life to which she was introduced was quite different from that to which she had been accustomed. There was a good deal more to its fulfillment than just attending services.

On Sunday afternoon, the Young Adults (and Washington was full of such employed as secretaries and subalterns of government) would go out in teams to visit the shut-ins; or to

St. Elizabeth's Hospital, where they would play games or just chat with the mental patients. Often afterwards they would come to the parsonage for sandwiches and cake. A crackling fire on the hearth made just the right setting to draw out their experiences of that afternoon or even questions as to the Christian life which had been in their minds. Besides this rapping there would be plenty of singing and laughter. Agneta loved these happenings and quickly became a constant in the group. So interested did she become in church life in America that she decided to terminate her housekeeping job and instead give herself as a volunteer to Augustana's program. She often accompanied Clarence on his hospital and shut-in calls and attended the various group meetings to get a well-rounded picture of the whole of an American pastor's role. And during these months she made her home with us.

How she endeared herself to the aging. Nor was the endearment confined to them! She became a well-loved participant in all young adult activities. An unforgettable scene comes to mind as staged at the front of our parish hall and church. We were about to take her to the airport for her return to Sweden. A large group of her friends gave a farewell party. As she was getting into our car, there was almost a struggle for her hand luggage between two young men who had been competing for her affection. One was a dashing young pastor from a suburban church; the other was a student from India, straight and tall, of the Brahmin caste. He too had become a member of the Youth Group and also shared a room in our home. The amazing thing was Agneta herself. Here she was returning to her homeland and family from whom she had been separated for this long year. She was weeping unrestrainedly because of the pain of parting from these new friends. In short, it was quite an experience for us all.

Bread returned?

We were privileged to visit Agneta's home a few years after her return. It was in a rural town called Molndahl, beautiful in its setting on a rocky wooded hillside. Her father was a retired schoolteacher, and her mother the soul of goodness and housekeeper-cook par excellence! We learned how Agneta had come back to her homeland determined to bring into her church the people-to-people concern she had experienced while in America. She enrolled at Uppsala university and graduated with a degree in theology, fully trained as a parish worker. But even while attending school she spent vacations working in a home for the aging. When she took us to visit this lovely place, it wasn't hard to see the endearment of these people for this girl of the loving heart. Their surroundings and physical comforts had always been first class. But here was one who brought another dimension to their living as she shared her faith and lived it in compassionate concern.

She also became a leader of a youth camp program which brought groups of Swedish youth into other countries—a hands across the seas program. They put their young shoulders to work in helping rebuild churches and homes in the war-devastated areas of Europe.

She spurred these youth on to serve rather than just be entertained. What an example they were to their elders! For many of them, church had become just an institution. It was startling then to find their young people, alive for Christ and witnessing to this new life by taking on the burdens of the less fortunate.

Agneta was aware of the Chicago inner city work in which our son David and our daughter Mary were engaged. She so challenged her Swedish young people that they adopted Chicago C A M (Christian Action Ministry) as one of their causes and sent generous offerings to help with that program. Agneta herself returned to spend a summer as a C A M staff worker in that west side ghetto.

How amazingly complicated is the returning of the bread sometimes! When our daughter Biz was to be married in Stuttgart, Germany, Agneta flew down from Sweden to be her attendant. She stood substitute for Mary, Biz' sister. Mary was then teaching in a girls' school on the slopes of the Kilimanjaro Mountain in Tanzania. We came from far off Saudi Arabia, where my husband served as a pastor in the oil community of Dhahran at the edge of the great desert. Our Washington church's choir director rode a night train from Paris where a government errand had him for the moment so that he might grace that service with his beautiful voice. And our Biz and Walle were from Indonesia. That truly was an international wedding.

Today Agneta is the wife of a Swedish clergyman and mother of two beautiful children. But her Christ-invaded heart continues to reach beyond her own little circle to the needs in her community and in the world.

What a return for the little investment of hospitality!

An Old Soldier's Crust

Not always does bread on the waters return with visible or material gain. But Mr. Frick, Spanish-American War veteran and guest of the U.S. Soldiers' Home in Washington, D.C. is an instance when it did.

Mr. Frick was a retired Swedish builder and lived in Washington. He literally "came out of the woodwork" when the Augustana church of that city sponsored the visit of the Crown Prince of Sweden. Newspaper publicity brought it to the attention of our old soldier. So he joined other Swedes for the festive worship that Sunday morning. And early that following week he visited the pastor having brought with him his Swedish baptism and confirmation "attest." He asked to be made a member of the family of God in the nation's capital.

By the time we came to Augustana Mr. Frick had moved over to the Old Soldiers' Home not far from Augustana church. Some of the buildings were post Civil War vintage. In fact a very historic building was a little cottage that served President Lincoln as a vacation spot for his family when summer's heat became oppressive. Mr. Frick, now enfeebled and unable to make it on his own to church, was on our list of shut-ins. Clarence tried to look in on him on a monthly basis. His dormitory building was one of the oldest. Built of limestone it had a running veranda with trellis-work of iron that encircled the whole of it.

It wasn't always easy to find this crochety old man since he was wont to stroll when the weather was inviting. And these grounds covered acres. In fact a herd of Holsteins pastured here. And there even was a tiny lake nestling among the trees and the sweep of green. Clarence might find him in the library or even in the snack shop for a coffee break.

He would reminisce about those first years in America as a greenhorn Swede. Jobs were hard to find. For one winter he found shelter in a cave working for a farmer and was paid by offerings of potatoes, a bit of salt meat and flour stone-ground at the nearby mill. And when there was work the pay was preposterously low. They took advantage of these newcomers and their bosses drove them mercilessly in the broiling summer sun. Cheap wooden houses, one almost touching the other, sprang up as their hammers sounded. No wonder that the great fire was to destroy Chicago completely as it roared from block to block. But out of those ashes was to rise a new city. And work was plentiful and wages mounted. It was then Mr. Frick became his own boss hiring others of his countrymen to do the work.

Now he could think of starting his own home. And he found a young woman who had come from the same part of the old country. Working in the home of a wealthy family she had sought out a Swedish church that catered to these recent arrivals by holding Sunday night fellowships. There they had met and soon Mr. Frick was building his own home. They "nested in" and a son was born to them.

Then came the Spanish-American War. Caught in the surge of war fever and telling himself that he owed it to this country which had already put him on such good footing, Mr. Frick enlisted. Then his story told of green troops being herded on ships hardly knowing how to fire the guns that were pressed into their hands. There were the marches through the fetid jungles, the spoiled rations of corn beef palmed off by greedy quartermasters, the bouts with malaria. But he was tough and so he eventually got back home to his family. And once again he could get back to contracting and as he put it, "I did all right!"

His son now had a family of his own and by all counts was doing well. But what was bitter bread for the old father was the complete rejection he now experienced. His wife had been laid to rest and now he was left all alone. "I don't even get as much as a Christmas card any more. And if my son stopped by to see me, I'd fall dead from shock."

Mr. Frick's health began to fail and from time to time he would be hospitalized. But no matter how difficult it was for him to get about he would painfully make it to the church office. He would demand to be alone with Clarence and then would pull out his "bale" of bills saying: "Please keep this 'junk' for me until I'm able to be on my feet again." He would tell Clarence the amount. After checking it against the roll Clarence would deposit it in the wall safe of the church. And usually he would add, "Now I hope no sticky fingers will touch this in the meantime."

I enjoyed inviting this lonely old man out of his barracks setting. On his birthday I would fix a celebration dinner at our house complete with a festive cake with his name and candles. In the meantime Clarence would pick him up by car. His old-country gallantry would come to the fore as I took his hand to welcome him at the door and he would lift mine to his lips.

Always he would protest saying, "Madame, you've gone to a lot of fuss for a mean old man." After the meal we would sing together some of the old familiar Swedish songs. I would draw him out as to boyhood memories back in Sweden and Clarence would have a *tänkespråk* out of Scripture and a prayer just special for Mr. Frick.

Then came what was to be his final hospitalization. His kidneys were malfunctioning and only the so-called "block-busters" sufficed to rid him of the gathering fluids. Food tasted like sawdust. He wearied of life and wanted out of this old world. He refused the pills so necessary if the breath of life was to continue in his frail body.

Strangely enough an order of Catholic nuns ministered in this government hospital. The obscene language and threatening acts of some of these ailing old men had made the turnover of younger nurses so rapid as to call for a radical change if this institution was to keep its doors open. So a contract had been let with this order of nuns. The stiffly starched garb and cross they wore demanded respect and they got it. But Mr. Frick had a strong bias. When his nurse saw that the pills were not being accepted she would ask him to open his mouth and then quickly push a pill down his throat. Usually he would gag and then she'd have a sip of water ready to wash it all the way down. But foxy Mr. Frick, despite his weakness, had one weapon left in his arsenal. The next time the nun's finger was in his mouth he bit it. And we are told that a human bite is every bit as poisonous as that of a mad dog. As a result all medications were taken away. And in two or three days Frick was dead.

But it should be inserted here that a few weeks earlier Mr. Frick had called Clarence to bring a lawyer to his bedside. He wanted to make his will. "Augustana is to have what I've got left," was his simple request. Clarence pleaded with him to remember his only son and not to carry that bitter feeling to his grave. Grudgingly he acquiesced, and it was arranged for the boy to have the first thousand dollars with the rest going to the church.

Frick was given a soldier's burial. His body was borne to its grave in the Old Soldiers' Home Cemetery on a gun caisson pulled by two white horses. The last note of the bugler and the thunder of the volley of guns had hardly died out when the son made his quick departure. He had not the slightest interest in the personal effects of his father. None of us ever did learn what had estranged this father and son. Here were feelings so intense that not even death could rub them out.

Once Clarence and I heard Little Mother Barnard witness

to a hall full of hungry cold men how God had Minneapolis Union Gospel Mission on his heart. This little woman, the wife of a successful surgeon, would leave her home each night to stand at the door and shake hands with these rejects of society and give them an encouraging word. This time she was recalling for them the time when the mission's mortgage was due, there weren't funds at hand, and foreclosure seemed certain. "Then it was," she went on to say, "we went to our knees in prayer. And do you know what? God keeps exact books. On the due date the response by mail put money enough to the last penny to cover that payment. And strangely enough, it also stopped with that. God does keep exact books!"

Such an experience happened again. The city had refused to issue a permit for Augustana's new educational building unless we could acquire an easement from the Roosevelt Hotel bringing our property to the alley line. And what Mr. Frick had left us in his will was just enough to acquire this "apple-pie slice" of land.

Again, here was "bread on the waters" and just enough too!

Amal Boody

During our stay in the Arabian Desert God put many interesting people across our path. Amal Boody, a Syrian nurse, surely stands out in this group.

She literally took her light from under the bushel and put it on the stand for all to see. And since she worked in the large Aramco Hospital at Dhahran doctors and fellow nurses as well as her patients got to see the light she carried deep within. She was a part of a dedicated nursing corps ready for any emergency in an oil pumping community where machinery could mangle, and open fires in the tents could sear. Many, like her, loved the Lord and theirs was a service with a plus. Others had seen much of life's nitty gritty, and without the gentle Holy Spirit's work within, had grown brittle and worldly.

Amal was a Syrian Christian. For years she had nursed a dream that one day she could open her own mission hospital deep in an unreached part of the Great Desert. She was sure to attend every worship to drink in the life-giving Word. Do you wonder that she became like one of our family? So when our Mary came to visit en route to her Tanzania assignment, a beautiful friendship developed between them.

Amal availed herself of every opportunity to study the Bible. Every Monday evening a group met at one of the worker's homes for book study directed by a lay teacher. It was an impressive sight to see these engineers and their wives, secretaries and nurses and others share the Word. Again every Friday when our church school was in session, one of the School's annex buildings would be used for a Bible class. In our church center, once each month secretaries and nurses employed in the Company Administration Headquarters or in the Aramco Hospital gathered for a luncheon I prepared. After the meal there would be a fast-moving Bible presentation. Lunch and Bible study lasted no more than an hour so they could go back to the job. Amal attended these for growth and encouragement.

One young medic made it his business to taunt Amal about her religion. He was a brilliant internist but an atheist. He seemed to find pleasure in seeking out Amal at the coffee break to make her the butt of his jibes at Christianity. He would ask the usual questions, "If Adam and Eve were the first humans on earth, where did Cain and Abel, their sons, procure their wives?" Or this old herring, "If God is love and all-powerful what do you make out of a child of praying parents being struck down with crippling polio?" Amal's quiet and thoughtful answers of faith must have searched out the chinks in his armor of unbelief as we shall afterward see. Maybe his derisive laughter was purely a covering. After all there is that promise of God: "My Word will not go forth and return void . . ."! And isn't our God a gentleman of the strictest honor, a gentleman who will never go back on his word?

There had been that farewell party for Mary before she was to continue on to Africa. We were clearing the dishes and straightening up when Amal asked the time of Mary's plane departure the next morning. I said, "Amal, don't even give it a thought! We'll be bringing her to the airport at 5:30 A.M."

"But I intend to be there to wave goodbye," was Amal's response. "Would you mind too much stopping for me?"

We knew there was no winning of that argument and agreed to take her along, knowing that we would be crowded in our little "bug" with Mary's loaded suitcases.

It was still dark when we left the house and signed out at the gate to head for Dhahran's beautiful new airport. The design was by the famous Yamasaki, a Japanese-American, and had cost some four million dollars. We soon covered the six miles across the stretch of beige sand and pulled up under the graceful arches. As Mary presented her ticket, the purser added, "But where is your visa?" It was my turn to panic and so I spoke up, "But I thought these were automatically sent up by Aramco's travel desk?" "Well," came his retort, "did you fill out the proper forms last week to remind them of her departure time?" Being very new I had to admit that I had failed to comply with this rule. "But she has to board this plane to make her connections in Tanzania. Folks will have driven miles to meet this plane. What can I do at this moment?" He only shrugged his shoulders to say, "I'm sorry, but there's absolutely nothing I can do!"

Seeing a high company official among those preparing to board the plane I told him our plight and he too could only add, "You have my regrets, but there is nothing to be done but wait for the next plane later in the week. There is no one in the company headquarters building we can rouse at this early hour."

Then Amal spoke up, "But I happen to know the head of the travel bureau. I'm a close friend with his wife. I'll ring him right now!" And without even asking for a telephone book she dialed the number and presently a sleepy voice was on the other end expressing amazement that someone would be arousing him from deep sleep. But he surely snapped to attention when Amal told her story and answered, "I'll pull on my trousers at once, get that visa out of the files, and then take it to the airport. In the meantime do your best to hold the plane!"

There we stood under the graying skies looking across the drab sand hoping against hope that the next car to show would be his. The Pan Am expediter was with us, nervously ticking off the minutes before he would have to signal the waiting ship to take to the air. But when the minutes dragged out he finally said, "Well, folks, this is it—departure time is already five minutes behind us. I can't hold up this international flight any longer. Even as it is I'm likely to be given a scratch on my record."

At that moment I turned to this Arab employee, and assuming he was a Moslem said, "Please, please, five minutes more! I know Allah will bless you for it!"

His answer was a shrug of the shoulder but he did delay still longer. A few minutes later he turned on his heel and started for the concourse. Just then we saw the feeble headlights of the little car moving at high speed on the last stretch. I ran to meet our kind friend, grabbed the visa which he held out of the window, and, catching up with the purser, thrust it into his hands. He stopped momentarily as the necessary rubber stamp was applied to it and then ran for the ramp with Mary at his heels. In a trice they were up the stairs and she was in the hands of the waiting stewardess while the purser made the last checkout with the plane's officers. The passengers had learned of Mary's predicament and gave her a rousing cheer. They were ever so happy that she had made it against impossible odds. This was bread from Amal's hand coming back to bless us all.

Not long afterwards Amal was taking a plane for London. She had registered for a course of mid-wifery in a world-famous center there. Letters from her told us of many difficulties she had to overcome. She was unprepared for the cold professionalism that marked an English hospital and the rigidity of their rules. More than once she was tempted to throw in the sponge and get back to her job at Dhahran. But there was this dream she had cherished all these years. And happily she did find some true friends who helped her past these hurdles. She found a warm Christian fellowship and it breathed new life into the years she spent in London. It was a great day when she held in her hands the diploma of graduation.

And she immediately set about to gather the needed supplies to equip her tiny hospital for new mothers. She chose to make her way to Quattar of Arabia where as yet little help was available for women in childbirth. Friends helped her find instruments and supplies. Even the oil company saw to it that equipment considered surplus from their well equipped hospital was taken by their planes to the airfield near the site of her clinic.

Mary and Amal correspond even to this day. They compare notes on their work, Mary in a Chicago ghetto and Amal deep in the desert of Arabia. How could these folks have come to meet and enrich each other's lives except as they were led by an unseen hand?

Doctor and
Internist of Dhahran

Those Aramco doctors in the Middle East were a breed apart. Dedicated as they were to their profession they joined this to their drive for adventure and had come out to work for Aramco in Arabia's "Great Desert." Some were devoted family men and welcomed this post as giving opportunity to have more relaxed time with their families and to share the lives of their children while advancing in their profession.

One of the most youthful among them had come highly recommended as an internist specialist. A brilliant medical career seemed to be opening up for him. He had come with his wife and three sons, and he was devoted to them, but when it came to religion he would have none of it. He considered himself above the need of any "crutch" as he was wont to dub what we call Christian faith.

But the very fact that he would go out of the way to ridicule others who devoutly believed made one to wonder if he might not be covering a fierce deep down struggle to believe. Isn't that the way some interpret St. Paul's stance as an arch-persecutor of the faith? He was trying with everything he could muster to silence the cry from deep within to believe. In one church a squirming worm is carved on the marble pavement just where the pastor stands at the altar when he leads the prayers of his people. With the weapons of prayer and the Word and Sacrament he literally heels under the old serpent, but the serpent never really stops wriggling. Only a stoutly held faith can finally win that victory.

Yet Amal Boody with her beautiful faith was more than a match for this doctor. He would twit her with "Amal, you seem to be on personal terms with the Almighty. Have you ever seen him?" To which her answer would come back, "Indeed I have, with the eyes of faith. I moreover know his Son Jesus, and Jesus is the spitting image of God as he said, 'He who has seen me has seen the Father.' "

At another coffee break he swaggered up to her, "Look at the long centuries Christianity has been in the world and then look at the mess we're still in." To this her answer was, "You remind me of the heckler in London's Trafalgar Square who with a dirty face had made fun of a Salvationist using these same words. And do you know what the quiet old Salvation Army man's word to him was?"

"I'd be interested in your telling me, Amal," said the doctor.

"Well, sir, it was this: 'Fella, look at the many eons water has been in the world and then look at the condition of your face.' "

"Christ hasn't failed," Amal went on to say. "We've failed to apply his timeless truths."

Usually Amal would conclude her confabs with the doctor by adding: "And doctor, I'm praying for you that God will yet be permitted to get through to your needy heart!"

And then he would add before turning away, "Well, Amal, I can't very well stop you from that!"

But with all this as a prelude what a complete surprise awaited us late that night when our doorbell rang. Here was Doctor "A" silhouetted against the dark of the night in his white uniform. "Excuse me for coming at so late an hour, but I've got trouble, bad trouble, and one of my colleagues suggested I seek you out for counseling. He agreed that I ought not postpone since I shared with him some of the dark thought I've entertained."

He then said that he'd thought of putting his whole family to sleep with poison. His story had to do with a grievous change in the relationship with his wife. She claimed he had stifled her love by neglect and total disregard of family for the concerns of his profession. She threatened to pick up the family and fly home saying that divorce was the only out. After he finished his story his whole body was torn with stifled sobs.

"As a doctor I know perfectly well I could tip over at any time, and frankly I'm frightened. I know I could lose control of myself and not be responsible. Oh, I need your help and the help of God Almighty."

While he was talking to Clarence I made coffee and sandwiches. The doctor admitted that he had not eaten that entire day and the informal discussion over that cup of coffee broke the tension.

Then followed a solid hour of searching the Bible together. Never did a heart reach more avidly for the great and comfortable promises of Scripture. Like Dag Hammarskjöld, this for Doctor "A" was the time his "Yes" was spoken to God. Clarence went to his home, so he could speak face to face with his wife and help them be reconciled with one another. Wisely she had determined that their home had to be built on a more solid foundation.

With the change in Doctor "A" came the most radical change of attitude of the whole medical staff. As Clarence made his regular bi-weekly hospital rounds he sensed that they had put him on the team. No longer did they look on him as an old witch doctor with a bag of charms and magic potions. We learned from a close confidant that Doctor "A" had openly spoken of how he'd been turned right about face from a terrible situation and helped to find "the better way." Now the doctors began to telephone Clarence to enlist his help with depressed patients. They would brief him about special needs of certain patients. The last months of chaplaincy there in faraway Arabia became a whole new thing.

Again here was "bread on the waters." Amal Boody in answer to prayer had found courage to speak of her faith to this seemingly hostile person and to persist against every discouragement. It is true, "My word shall not return void but will accomplish that whereunto I have sent it." That promise of God stands though heaven and earth pass away.

Arjun Chauhan-Indian Nurse

He calls us Dad and Mom, this dark skinned Indian nurse of Arjun. He was a highly respected member of the Protestant Fellowship we served those years in the Arabian Desert. He had been a member of a Mennonite community in India. His dark skin gave one to know that he had been won for Christ from among India's low caste peoples. Skillfully trained at a Christian hospital as a male nurse Arjun had taken employment at Aramco's Dhahran hospital. Since Saudi Arabia is the Moslem homeland it is unthinkable for women nurses to tend male patients.

One look at this kindly man in his crisp whites and you knew he rated high. Although short in stature his poise and erect bearing made him stand out in any crowd as one who had full confidence in his skills and who walked in peace with his God and fellow men. It was not to wonder at, then, that when King Ibn Saud became a patient at Aramco's hospital, Arjun was chosen to be his nurse. This in itself indicated the high respect Arjun enjoyed.

We came to know Arjun by his deep involvement in our Protestant Fellowship. He was there each Sunday evening as we gathered in the Company Movie Theater for our weekly worship. This huge building had seating for 600 or more but seemed to swallow up our modest congregation of 250 worshipers. The unadorned hall was severely functional. A high stage across the entire front made it difficult to transform the hall into a temple for the living God. We did the best we could. A small crudely fashioned altar would be wheeled out and then adorned with a cross and candles. A tryptych simulating three art glass windows was set up behind it. Usually someone with a good feel for flowers arranged bouquets of plastic blooms imported from Italy. And below the apron of the stage, the plywood pulpit was placed to the right and the Hammond electric organ to the left. The choir was seated between these. Both organist and choir director were volunteers from the ranks of the congregation. The congregation was truly ecumenical. Some 30 denominations were counted among its members.

Besides this mix from America were the 80 or more Indian Christians coming from Mar Thoma, Mennonite, and other Protestant groups in India. Among these Arjun stood out as a leader and was elected to the church council. He took his assignments with the rest of the elders, serving on committees that recommended the various missions which were to be supported and that planned the congregation's many-faceted activities. He taught Sunday school which was held on Friday, the Moslem Sabbath.

Arjun and other Indian nurses would gather each Saturday evening for a Bible study in their recreation building. Since Clarence and I conducted these studies we learned to know each of these fine people personally. When necessity arose it was natural that we turned to Arjun to fill in for us. He did this with great skill. He had a natural flair for illustrations out of life to make these texts come alive.

Arjun felt enough at home with us to drop in for a visit from time to time. There'd be that timid knock and the joy of meeting when the door opened to reveal this dear Christian outside. What beautiful conversations on the deep things of the Lord we had over a bite of lunch or a cup of coffee. This friendship was richly rewarding.

He flung wide the door to ever so many in the Indian community. When they brought family with them it meant they "lived on the economy." Housing was difficult at best at El Khobar, the Arab village just five miles from our oil community Dhahran. A water tap and a tiny sink plus a crude stove were the conveniences in the kitchen and the other rooms were cramped.

Arjun also enlisted the Indian children for Sunday school. At his suggestion a bus was hired to bring them in to the Fellowship Friday school. We encountered problems of communication but children quickly pick up the needed words. Some of the most beautiful pictures we gathered while in Dhahran were of these children as they participated in Christmas and Easter programs. Their mothers had dressed them in colorful "look alike" costumes.

When we teased Arjun about his remaining a bachelor with so many pretty and talented Indian nurses at hand he would smile and add, "Oh, my parents back home will work this out when they deem the time is ripe." And on one of those furloughs he accepted their choice for him as a dutiful son. They had negotiated with the parents of a daughter who had been educated as a lawyer. She did return with Arjun for one term in Arabia but declined thereafter to go back to that kind of isolation in a strange culture. She bore him children but put them in the care of her parents so as to be free to practice her profession. These long and unnatural separations work a real hardship for workers like Arjun and only their Christian commitment gave them the strength needed to carry on. Again the better pay would make possible the purchase of a home in India and also to see that their children were educated and properly launched in the arena of life. They were today's "Jacobs" who slaved long years to achieve flock and family.

The day arrived when we were to leave Arabia. Arjun was heavyhearted and acted like any son about to lose his parents. Of course he was at the official farewell reception which the community gave us. He knelt at that "Last Supper" celebration which climaxed our last worship. He also insisted on being with us at the airport just before we left, joining with the rest of our church family to sing "God Be with You Till We Meet Again." But he wanted a personal word and drew from his pocket a jewelers' box and asked us please to open. Here were cuff links fashioned with Saudi Arabia $25 gold pieces. When Clarence and I protested, "But Arjun, this is all too much!" his answer was, "Too much for Dad? Never!"

We had known another gold far more precious than the black gold big business is pumping from the subterranian depths of the desert. Ours was the gold of a tried and tested friendship in Christ. Our letters still cross one another and very often we lift up Arjun and his beautiful family to the throne of God for his blessing.

Bob Crabtree, Cherokee Indian

Somebody once asked Josiah Royce of Harvard, "What is your definition of a Christian?" The great philosopher answered, "I don't know how to define that. But wait," he added, looking out of his window. "There walks one in the person of Phillips Brooks!" Dr. Brooks was his definition on two legs.

Bob Crabtree, American Indian of the Cherokee tribe stands out in our minds as the best definition we know of a Christian steward on "two legs." We met him half way around the world in the desert of Saudi Arabia. He was one of 250 master sergeant technicians at the airbase just outside of Dhahran, the Armaco Oil community. Crabtree was a part of a remnant U.S. training force teaching Saudi Arabian counterparts airplane maintenance. Classified as a "hardship post" by the U.S. Air Force these men had been hand-picked for their jobs. They were for the most part family men who at this far place were two continents removed from loved ones. Plunked down in the heart of a desert with little to amuse themselves is it any wonder that utter boredom tore some of them to pieces?

Our Sunday night worship services became a "lifeline" for ever so many. Some volunteered for the choir and found the singing and happy camaraderie great medicine. All of them would be invited after services to our simple cement-block home for informal get-togethers. I would serve those big he-man sandwiches with slabs of roast beef or cheese and followed up with chocolate cake with thick gooey frosting. And there was cup after cup of "Swedish egg coffee" to wash it all down. I led the singing with my "uke." Others joined in by plucking guitars and autoharps. What great times we had together as men sang away their homesickness.

Many times these men have crossed our lives since and always it was to grip our hands as they poured out gratitude.

Once when Clarence and I were on a mission to Alaska for the military we heard a knock at the door of our guest quarters. When we opened it a man in a snappy uniform said, "You remember me?" And when we honestly had to confess that memory failed us he burst out, "I'm Moon Mullins! You saved my life out there in Arabia! I was about to go mad from homesickness. And then you opened your home to me as did others of your Christian congregation there and it changed everything. I made up my mind that as soon as I retired from the military I'd go to school and study to be a Baptist pastor. And now I'm serving my last year and I have already enrolled in that school." Soon we were being introduced to Moon's wife and precious family at that below-zero outpost of the far north.

But to get back to Bob Crabtree this was the story he told. He had been a rounder if there ever was one. One of the jobs he held illustrates perfectly how nail-hard and tough he really was. As an orderly in a mental hospital he was assigned to the criminal ward. Then he fell in love. The girl was a Christian and was all decided that hers would be a Christian home. Swept off his feet by her loveliness Bob did everything he knew to make sure that she'd be his. But as to her Christian commitment he gave only lip service. Then jobs became scarce. And soon after their marriage, Bob was walking the streets hoping against hope for a break, but every door slammed shut for him.

Then his wife's faith really got to him. "God isn't dead," she said. "God is still in his heaven. Bob, let's you and I get on our knees and really ask him to help. Doesn't he tell us that his eye is on the sparrow?" Then it was that Bob caved in. With sobs he prayed God to forgive his "robber years" (as he was wont to call them remembering the penitent thief on the cross) and most of all for his stony heart of unbelief.

That very next day he got a small job. It paid him $10. Sunday followed next and he and his wife went to church together. Bob put $1 on the plate at which his wife whispered, "Bob, couldn't you wait with the tithe until we see what's ahead?" Bob's answer, "But I promised God!" Their faith was sorely tried more than once thereafter but Bob would add in conclusion, "Looking back, that was the beginning of all our blessings."

It's many years ago back in Duluth that Clarence and I began our lifelong habit of tithing. We take our stand right alongside of Cherokee Bob to witness to the unnumbered blessings received. "Man," objected a pal to his tither friend, "you're crazy giving so much. First thing you know you'll have nothing for yourself." "That'll never happen," came the answer back, "for as fast as I shovel out, God shovels in. Only God's got a bigger shovel." Last year I was called by the Internal Revenue Service to have my income tax reviewed. They thought our giving to be vastly padded and asked that I bring documentary evidence to support the figures. As I flashed those receipts one by one it was my turn to witness to the blessings which had accrued to us in that giving.

Our Lord puts it in simple terms: "Give and it shall be given to you." Let's think of our need to give. How else is that death-grip of things to be broken? What better time than now to begin earnestly to stash up treasures in heaven where moth and rust do not destroy or thieves break in to steal?

And then you'll join Bob Crabtree to watch the loaves pile in on life's wide shore.

General Peter Sing

What a privilege has been ours to have the opportunity of relating with people around the world! And because many were on temporary assignments by their governments or their business firms, they were separated from families and appreciated all the more the hand of fellowship and the open door of hospitality. We were always twice blessed!

A shining example of this in our Geneva experience was Peter. Loyal Christian that he was, he sought out our little church at the heart of "old town." He was a humble man and although he entered into the worship with all his heart he remained close-lipped about his errand in Switzerland for his country, the Republic of China in Taiwan.

That first Sunday we invited him home to dinner. He took a great interest in our library. We love sharing books and have accepted the fact that a book on loan might never return. But Peter always brought his back and each week we would choose another one or two to carry back to his rented quarters. But since we kept no record on those borrowed there was one he held back for an unusually long time. Then when he returned it, he said somewhat apologetically, yet with a wide grin on his face, "Forgive me for keeping this book so long. But maybe you will be pleased to know that I have translated it into Chinese so that my friends back home can read this thrilling story too!" The book was *Monanga Paul,* the story of the life and tragic murder of Dr. Paul Carlson who as a physician had labored untiringly in the Congo of Africa only to be senselessly slaughtered with others herded into the large square at the heart of the city. But the book makes one know again that the blood of the martyrs is indeed the seed of the church.

Interestingly enough this book was afterward published in Taiwan. I have seen a copy of it and was amazed that on the jacket cover was an enlarged photo of the collage my husband had fashioned from chards which we gathered from rubbish heaps of ancient villages in the sands of Saudi Arabia. The broken pieces make up a design of rare beauty: A large chalice formed from beige chards and outlined by broken bits of blue glass bracelets stands on a globe of Persian blue. And from beads and tiny shells and a bit of acid-eaten coin the symbols of the fish, and the Rose of Sharon and the Lily of the Valley help tell the story.

In our apartment each Sunday evening we had a fellowship group to study the Word and to seek God's will for our lives in prayer. The group included missionaries from Tanzania, now working at headquarters in Geneva; a Swiss engineer and his British wife who had served some 20 years in India; a woman from Russia; a fine young couple from Norway of which the husband was a scientist with CERN (an international atomic research group); an American nuclear scientist and his wife, also with CERN, and others. Peter became a part of this vital spiritual fellowship.

We never truly learned how much all this meant to him until the morning of our departure for the states. We were driving to Le Havre, France, to board a boat for our transatlantic crossing. Our missionary friends, the Elmer Danielsons, had invited us for breakfast in their apartment. It was set at an early hour since we had miles to go and wanted a good start. Imagine our joy, when who should show up to bid us good-bye but Peter Sing! His moving words of appreciation were recalled many times along the journey and we were floored with the generous content of the envelope he slipped into our hands as we got into the car. It all seemed in reverse —for we were the ones who had been blessed by his friendship.

You can understand how overwhelmed we were recently to receive a letter from our foster son in Taipei that brought Peter back on the horizon of our lives again. The letter tells its own story. Writes Paul T. M. King:

> We have in Taipei a Sunday Fellowship of Christians who gather for witness and prayer. The man who is chiefly responsible for this activity is our capable Minister of Finance, Mr. K. T. Li. Lillian and I are wont to attend. Yesterday evening we had a Mr. Sing and the title to his witness was, "We Must Live the Scriptures." As he began his testimony he read from Acts 20:17-38. Then he began to tell us that many years back he was sent by the government to engage in some undercover work in a French-speaking country. He said that the pastor and his wife were both kind to him. He could find all the good Christian virtues in their daily living, and he was greatly touched by their love. This alone made his work and living in a strange land bearable. But the time had come for the American pastor and his wife to leave to go to Chicago where they had accepted a call. Then he described in the most moving words how he parted from them with tears. The pastor's wife called him her son although she was at most 10 years his senior. At this point it became suddenly clear to me who this American couple was. They had to be the Nelsons of my life too! And of course, this Mr. Sing should be General Peter Sing, whom you had mentioned to me some years ago but whom I had failed to locate.
>
> After the testimony, I introduced myself to him.

He knew my name long ago. So we finally met. Mr. Sing is now an elder and works full time for a Lutheran congregation affiliated with the church of Norway. . . . What a dramatic setting for our meeting. . .

Bread upon the waters—returned a thousandfold!

High School Tripper

She crossed our path when we were serving our Lord in Geneva, a world crossroad. Not only international organizations, but also prestigious schools are located here. The Swiss have an image of being a conservative and well-disciplined people and this image has led rich parents to send their pampered and overindulged kids to school here so they could learn to toe the mark and shape up.

But after many contacts with some of the students we learned that you can lift the kids out of "deviltry" and our permissive society but you can't be so certain that once out of sight and in another's hands you have them safe and out of reach of the demons loose in today's society.

Youth often like to dramatize their escapades and paint them in the most lurid colors, but our informers came from a random sampling of these schools. We often played host to one or the other of them whose parents had been affiliated with our Protestant Fellowship in Dhahran of Saudi Arabia. They were full of talk and so we did get what we thought was a clear picture of life at these schools. In some of the boys' schools clandestine fraternities sprang up and as an initiation each member had to go through obscene sexual activity to prove his manhood. In girls' schools they told wild stories of pulling the wool over the proctor's eyes for a "free" night on the town. The hardest to believe was that the drug cult had reached its long fingers into these out-of-the-way mountain crossroads. I must narrate this experience just the way it happened.

The girl had been our house guest in Geneva, brought there by her roommate, a girl whose family was very dear to us from those Arabian Desert days. This particular girl's parents, now divorced, were professional people in a Midwest American city. The mother was a distinguished psychiatrist. No doubt about it, the girl had an unusually bright mind. That she was a "spoiled brat" just couldn't be debated. Her every whim had been catered to. She had her own car back home, a gift which came probably loaded with the parents' inner guilt feelings for having had so little personal time to give her. Her only brush with religion was a white Bible her maternal grandmother had put in her hands the day she graduated from grade school. I so well recall her comment after our Sunday dinner. We had dined taking time to flavor the food, and the conversation at the table had been fascinating as one question or another drew them out. She said, "This is the first time I ever sat down to an organized dinner with adults!"

She was full of questions about our faith, the "whys" and "wherefores" of Baptism and Communion and other church practices. In the give and take that afternoon time was pushed to the back of the stove. Then after an evening snack we drove her to the railway station where she boarded the trigger-trim mountain express.

A month or two later Clarence received a telephone call. It was the school counselor. "Pastor, would you be so kind as to meet the afternoon train? Shirley will be aboard. She is to depart about an hour later for America. We can't risk her being at loose ends even for an hour. Her parents will meet the plane in New York and bring her home for a rest." That was all of it. There just was no time to flesh out the details of what had happened.

85

Clarence had no difficulty picking her out of the crowd pouring onto the platform when the train pulled up. By reason of their dress and free and easy ways Americans stand out in any crowd on a foreign place. Soon they were chatting merrily as if setting out for a picnic or a ski trip. He had to notice how her eyes ferreted out every young male and how easy it was for her to exchange pleasantries with total strangers. Then she briefed him on her own jolting experience.

She had been snared by marijuana and had popped the "pep pills." In a fit of depression during a hangover she had sought to cop out of life. Everything had looked sick and gray. While in that mood she'd managed to pulverize a very thin wine glass and had ingested it with her food. However, she confided in her roommate who had the sense to sound the alarm with the school authorities, and in minutes a doctor had pumped her stomach. She seemed almost proud that she had the guts to carry through on this attempt at self-destruction.

There remained less than a half hour when finally she was checked in at the airport. Clarence had been praying for guidance to choose his words carefully. He knew that he had to play for the high stakes of a complete turnover of her life to Jesus Christ. She listened, as if her life depended on every word. Her ticket in hand, the flight announced, she flung her arms about Clarence to say good-bye as she said, "I'll be thinking over what you said while crossing the Atlantic."

Again it was bread on the waters. Clarence and I reflected, "Will we ever hear from her again?" Months later we received a letter. We could only marvel as we read. She had indeed "come to herself." Those first days at home she had great difficulty sleeping. "I was turning over everything that had happened in the light of your words, Pastor. I knew it wouldn't do to make my life nice on the outside. It had to be good all the way through. All new!" Then she wished she might have a direct word from God and remembered the white Bible her grandmother had given her. It took some searching in the late night hours to find it tucked away with other books, but she did locate it. Triumphantly she let it open where it would and read the first verse her eye came to rest on. It was 1 Chronicles 22:19: "Now set your mind and heart to seek the Lord!"

It was God speaking to her. Now the scattered fragments of her life began to pull together much like the filings are pulled into a pattern by a magnet. Her life had to count for something. Yes, for God! And so that very next morning she got busy seeking out a meaningful job in a home for retarded children. She then told of how she had set her goal to serve special children and was arranging the schooling necessary to prepare her. She hunted up a Christian church where her faith could be nourished. "All the while I was bubbling over with happiness. The Lord was affirming each step!" Do you wonder that our hearts too were singing over there in Geneva?

Our "tripping friend" had stumbled on to the truth "that a loaf is only a half a loaf unless we share it."

Our Grown Daughter, Lorraine

What unexpected returns often arise out of simple responses!

Perhaps the beginning of this story goes back to my school teacher days. Often as a Christian I was called on to give my witness to young people's groups and church forums. A series of six such Sunday evening groups at First Lutheran in St. Paul somehow got into my date book one fall. I can still recall the fun I had in planning the series under the overall theme, "The Treasure Hunt." It gave me a chance to explore the Christ in the field of literature, in the field of painting and sculpture, in the field of music; and from there on in a search for him in the office, in the classroom, in the factory, on the street. It was a challenging assignment, and besides I loved the opportunity to make new friends.

As the word went out, young folks from neighboring churches joined the group. That sizable social room was well filled with eager, enthusiastic youth. Little did I realize that two of those in attendance were to play a very large part in my life. One became our foster daughter.

Lorraine was just 12 years old when her beloved, beautiful Christian mother was found to have cancer. Her father and mother had emigrated from Sweden and had established their home in St. Paul. A skilled craftsman and carpenter, the father was doing very well. Two children were born to bless the family, a son Walter, and daughter Lorraine. When these children were in their early adolescence this cancer struck without warning. In later years Lorraine told of how her mother didn't want the children to see her in those last weeks of excruciating pain just before her death. In those days the medical profession knew so little what to do. Cancer research was just beginning. But this mother was not a fair-weather Christian. Through all the pain and tribulation she trusted the Lord, and by believing prayer, gave her family into his almighty hands. The priceless treasure of her faith has come to fruit in the lives of her children. I have often thought that it could have been those mother's prayers that brought us into their lives. A year after the mother's death, the father died. All their relatives were in Sweden and Norway; to whom then should they go?

But I'd better get back to the school teacher. That next summer after my Treasure Hunt series, at a youth camp on Lake Independence, I met the State President of the Youth Leagues, one Clarence Nelson. After a three-mile swim across the lake, we became more than just friends. The next summer the wedding bells rang, and on our wedding day, through the mails there came a call to serve the Arlington Hill Lutheran Church in St. Paul. Previous to this time, Clarence had been serving the Mt. Olivet Lutheran Church in South Minneapolis. From the Arlington Church came Lorraine and her bosom friend Arlene to the Treasure Hunt series. We accepted the call and on December 1 we began our home building in the Phalen Park area.

Clarence plunged into the work of fanning the fires of faith in a congregation made up largely of skilled workers. These were very hard hit by "the Great Depression" of the mid-'30s. I soon found myself teaching Bible to the previous year's confirmation class. Here I met Lorraine and Arlene. I remember coming home after those first Sundays with this class and saying to my husband, "There is something that deeply moves me about Lorraine Servheen. If ever the opportunity came, I'd love to take her into our home as a daughter." I was to learn later that after one of those Treasure Hunt Sunday meetings, Lorraine had confided to her friend, Arlene, "You know I have a feeling that woman is going to mean something in my life" (and this was before I had even met my husband).

About one year later, when our firstborn was a wee baby, a telephone call came from Lorraine and Walter's family doctor whom the court had appointed guardian. "Can you help me?" he asked my husband, "I must find a home for the Servheen children. The place where they have been staying no longer has room." Putting his hand over the phone's mouthpiece, Clarence relayed the message to me. "Tell him we'll take them," I said, and as quickly as that, a decision was made that brought untold blessings to our lives. Lorraine and Wally came to live with us. A bit of rearranging of bedroom space and we had them settled in.

But in another year, our firstborn was to have a brother, and we found a splendid home for Wally just a block away. In this home lived one of his high school pals. But Wally did have Sunday dinner with us so that brother and sister could keep a warm and intimate tie.

And Lorraine? Words are inadequate to describe the blessing she has been to us! She worked her way through college, some summers acting as housekeeper for a wealthy family in White Bear. I'll never forget when she was starting out for college how she came to me and said, "Ruth, what about the things I won't be taking with me?" My answer, "Why, you're to leave them here, of course! This is your home for always!" Then breaking into sobs, she put her arms around me and said, "You have no idea what that means to someone who wouldn't otherwise know where to go!"

Those rich years we were blessed by sharing her college friends, and having a daughter come home at Christmas, and the children having a big sister whom they looked up to and dearly loved.

Out of college, she became my brother Reuben's first parish worker at Mt. Olivet. She made her calls on a bicycle. Those were the lean years in a church that was staging a come-back after a depression in which it had lost everything. Later she received a call to go into student work on the Iowa State Campus and later still at Iowa University. From those whose lives were changed by the infection of the Christ who lived within Lorraine, there have emerged some of the church's great leaders, not least among them the late Dr. Kent Knutson, who at the time of his passing was president of the American Lutheran Church.

Meanwhile, we had moved to Washington, D.C. We suggested that Lorraine come to live with us and seek some work there. We will never forget her busy, dedicated life. Besides holding her job in a National Youth Temperance Organization she plunged into the youth program at Augustana Church in that exciting setting. How she strengthened our work in every direction!

One day there came a call from a bachelor pastor whose parish was in Chicago. He had met Lorraine at a Student Ashham some time before. He was coming to Washington and wanted her to have lunch with him. I guess that's all it took. From that time on we had a starry-eyed gal in our home!

Several summers before, at our Sand Lake cabin, my brother Reuben had said, "Lorraine, you ought to get married!" She asked, "Who will it be?" He named off several very eligible young bachelor preachers to which she responded, "But Rube, there's no star dust!" His quick reply came, "Forget that star dust business!"

Well, when the engagement to Win was settled, she telephoned Rube from Washington. Her opening sentence was, "Rube, there is too star dust!" And in response to his startled, "What do you mean?" she announced her engagement.

Our whole family grew excited about the prospects of a wedding in the offing. And Lorraine's young brothers were eager to plumb the depths of her love to her betrothed. Their

$64 question was, "Lorraine, would you be willing to share your toothbrush with him?" Her only answer was a giggle.

That was a lovely June wedding in Augustana's cathedral-like church with Lorraine's two young sisters as junior bridesmaids. And somehow amidst the busyness of it all, I sensed her mother's presence and the beautiful answer to her faith-filled prayers.

She is a dedicated pastor's wife, mother of four gifted, fine children. That parsonage knows hospitality with a capital "H"! Open to the aging and the young, to folks from all walks of life and all shades of color, to anybody in need, it is blessed with the presence of the One who so plainly gave us the "inasmuch" directives!

What greater return could any parents have than to know their children love and serve the Lord! It's bread returned a hundred-fold. We opened our home; Lorraine has filled our hearts with joy!

Elsie Gibson,
Our Smoked Swede

She liked to dub herself, "Elsie, your smoked Swede daughter." We'd like you to know the girl behind that name. She came to us in Washington, D.C., just days after her plane from Guatemala had set down at the National Airport along the west shore of the muddy Potomac. She was met by her future employers, Judge and Mrs. Leventhal, and an old friend of Elsie's who herself had come earlier to find a job as a domestic. The Leventhals had forwarded the ticket.

From childhood Elsie had been a committed Christian, so it was natural that one of her first requests was about a church. Not long before this Augustana Church had been given newspaper publicity about its "Operation One Mile" program in which it had determined to invite anyone living in a radius of one mile to consider Augustana as their place of worship. There would be no distinction as to color. All were welcome and since integrated churches were almost non-existent in those days the newspapers had written up the story. The news article had called the judge's attention to our church. So his answer to Elsie was, "I know just the church for you and I'll drive you there myself tomorrow morning."

On the first Sunday she came to church it happened that

our daughter Mary was home for summer work in the post office. Mary noticed this black girl sitting all alone, so right after worship she took Elsie in tow and introduced her to other young adults. Mary had also taken note of the brilliant voice with which Elsie struck up the hymns that Sunday. These must have been familiar to her since there is nothing Elsie loves more than to "lift" a Gospel hymn. She became a "regular" at worship that summer and came to know many of the happy youth to whom that "little cathedral" at the foot of Meridian Hill Park was a spiritual home away from home.

By the time we returned from our vacation days in Minnesota Elsie was happy in her associations. She enjoyed the varied activities of these youth, an outdoor concert at Watergate or Carter Baron Theater, their outings to the mountains of Virginia and a weeknight of volleyball in the park. Before bringing her to meet us, Mary said, "Dad and Mom, you've just got to be family to Elsie. She has absolutely no one in the world to call kin. Oh, yes, there's that sick little woman in Costa Rica to whom she sends a monthly check as a 'thank you' for taking care of her after her mother died. Otherwise she's all alone. And remember she's in a strange new land."

Elsie was a child of love, but born out of wedlock. Her father was of Spanish blood and he wanted very much to marry that young mother, but the stubborn pride of her grandfather would have none of it despite the fact that he himself offered so little to his hardworking daughter in the rearing of this her only child. The home was hardly more than a shack, but Elsie loves to tell how each week that slivered pine board floor was scrubbed until it shone.

With her quick gifted mind it is no wonder that she excelled in school. But there were fees to be paid and when money didn't reach for food and clothes and school the teacher was asked to wait. This made him angry enough to beat little Elsie unmercifully in sight of the class. She ran home sobbing and vowed to her mother that she would never return. Elsie never finished grade school, but was put out to a well-to-do family in Guatemala to help in the kitchen. The family belonged to the Catholic Church and were kind and gentle to this growing child, and in turn she was attentive and helpful to them, all the while learning the art of cooking and cleaning. That one of the ladies was a partial invalid, we think, drew out the tenderness that Elsie expresses so well.

Elsie became active in the local Protestant church which unhappily suffered persecution from unthinking adherents of the majority faith. The persecution only served to ground Elsie even firmer in her faith. She found herself in the role as soloist at church services. She loves to describe the time she sang to thousands at a revival conducted in the stadium of a nearby city.

The day Elsie became a U.S. citizen was a red-letter day. I can close my eyes any time and see her in her chic dress making that pledge of allegiance before the judge and the audience of friends and family members of those taking the oath along with her. The Augustana Choir made a great occasion of it. And after the rehearsal at church that night choir members congratulated her with coffee and slices of a large cake each carrying a miniature U.S. flag. The overall inscription read, "Proudly We Salute You, Citizen Elsie!"

She liked to spend every Thursday at our home, and we had made a point of giving her a key. We had discovered that Elsie and three of her friends working as domestics rented a modest apartment so that they would have a place to be on their "days off." When I had to be away for an out-of-town speech or retreat Elsie took delight in fixing her special Guatemalan dish for dad.

There was the time I asked Elsie if she'd ever been mistreated because of her color. "Oh yes," she said, and that without a trace of bitterness. "The other Sunday as I waited on the corner for my bus, a car loaded with young men slowed in passing and shouted obscenities. I only pitied them and quietly prayed that they'd get to know the Christ I love."

What follows here you may find hard to believe, but it does prove that what we call the American dream is more than wishful thinking. When Clarence and I served the English-speaking Lutheran Church in Geneva, Elsie availed herself of a European tour. She was able to visit us in Geneva. We showed her the beauties of Geneva and drove her to Lucerne to rejoin her travel group. That stop was special to her and meant much to us.

Every summer Elsie spends her vacations with our family in the log cabin we have owned these 40 years and which is located on the shores of beautiful Sand Lake near Moose Lake, Minnesota. She's everyone's favorite. How she spoils our grandchildren and fattens us all baking up a storm of sour dough bread and luscious rolls. Each summer she integrates the little village and the church where we worship. Usually she giggles as she says, "Look, Mom, I was the only fly in the pan of cream today."

Elsie is proud of the condominium she is acquiring by monthly payments. On Thursdays and also on Sundays when she has free time she visits the sick and shut-ins in the home for aged. She loves her choir work and shows it by having them all up to her apartment for one of her tasty home-cooked meals. If you attend Augustana in Washington on a Sunday take note of the beautiful black woman singing in the choir, and like as not presiding as hostess at the after-church coffee hour.

Such times that Elsie is near one of the churches any of us serve, you may be sure she's called on to sing a solo. One Sunday she was with us at Tabor in Chicago. That neighborhood had changed almost overnight and many of the whites left had hangups about color. At first when Elsie began singing there was a stiffening in the audience. But as her beautiful voice rang out the stanzas of what was a favorite to many Swedes in the congregation, "Om jag agde alt men icke Jesus" ("If I gained the world but lost my Savior") she won them one by one. Every eye misted and hearts went out to her. At our family gatherings Dave gets reminded of the time he introduced Elsie at his church in Chicago, which is almost 100% black. He announced, "Elsie will now sing my favorite of all songs," and then in an aside to her he asked, "What's the name of it, Elsie?" Did he ever get razzed!

Here's one we all demand of her when she's with us. We call it Elsie's song:

> It is morning
>   It is morning in my heart;
> Jesus makes the gloomy shadows
>   All depart.
> For since Jesus is my king,
>   Songs of gladness now I sing.
> It is morning
>   It is morning in my heart.

Bread upon the waters! No blood parents are more faithfully remembered at the throne of mercy nor are they the recipients of greater gratitude than that this beloved daughter showers on us!

Heart Room
Equals Home Room

The years in Washington made for many an open door. Amazingly enough almost every time I address an audience someone is sure to clutch my arm afterwards and say, "Thanks for having my son to dinner while he was in the service and stationed near the nation's capital." Another might put it, "My daughter sang in your choir. How she appreciated those youth times at your home when after a hearty lunch you'd have them on the floor by the crackling fire for a sing." A maturely poised man will warmly take her hand and say, "You insisted we stop for dinner after church when I'd mentioned my name and that I was from Minnesota. And then you added, 'You've got the same name as our younger son.'" When Clarence was making visits at the Augustana Home for the Aged, a woman in a wheelchair asked, "Do you remember me? I was in the Augustana choir that day you first came from Duluth." And then she named off the four children. "I can see them as if it were yesterday, those darling children. You see, I worked at the War Department."

But the international contacts are a chapter all by themselves. These have indeed been "bread on the waters." When Clarence and I touched down in Taipei years later a cluster of these dear friends came to meet us. Each wanted us to be guests in their home or sought to settle on a date when we could be their dinner guests at some cafe.

Let me tell the story of Paul T. M. King. He is a son to us in the same way that Timothy was to St. Paul. St. Paul wrote of him. "Timothy, you are like a son to me in the things of the Lord" (1 Timothy 1:2). It all began with a letter from Miss Clara Jones, a missionary in Taipei. She wrote on behalf of one of her students who was soon to arrive in Washington to begin a year's study in government finance. The letter went on to say, "Paul is a new Christian and I fear lest being caught up in the Washington milieu he will lose touch with his faith. Could you recommend a Christian home where he can find supportive Christian fellowship and an introduction to a Christ-centered and lively church family?"

Clarence and I spoke in concert: "Why can't it be our home? We have room." Our family was away at school so their rooms stood unused. The bus on the corner would take him where he wanted to go. And Augustana had a wonderful mix of internationals. Moreover we had become an integrated congregation and color of skin and slant of eye meant less and less, thank God! So that day our letter was off by air mail welcoming Paul to our home.

He won us that very first day. Despite all he'd gone through he had a happy outlook. I can still hear his shuffle on the stair and cheerful morning greeting. Table conversations were ever so interesting and he took to American cooking like a duck to water. And when a soft-boiled egg was set before him he like as not would say, "I'm going to eat this like General MacArthur, with salt and black pepper." That he had a good mind was apparent when he was singled out for a special seminar under the famous economist, Dr. Walter Heller at the University of Minnesota. Dr. Heller even offered him a teaching fellowship at the conclusion of these studies. Paul turned this offer down since he had promised his government on leaving Formosa that he would plow back what he learned on whatever assignment they had for him on his return.

Paul was fluent in the use of English. He was popular with the youth at church and took part in all their many activities. He entered into the Sunday evening discussions with zest. He enjoyed the give-and-take of conversation at a nearby restaurant where the group often went to conclude their evening together.

Paul was married and had a family, but they had become separated when Paul had to flee for his life when the Japanese made their incursion into mainland China. He had been mayor of a large city and like as not would be marked for death. He had solemnly promised to do everything to reunite them once he had established himself. Finally the day came when arrangements were completed with agents in a type of "underground railway" with payment in advance. But the sad word came back that his wife refused to leave. She was a pediatrician and found employment with the communist government. No other explanation was offered. Little wonder that Paul began thinking that she may even have been "brainwashed." Again there was the possibility that she had remarried. But Paul persisted in the hope he would once again have his arms around his little family. He wrote them at regular intervals. One day his mail included a letter from the mainland. Now his step was on the stairs. Instead of light and tripping, his step was measured and heavy. He held the letter in his hand to read to us. With a voice of anguish he said, "There are only 46 words. She says for me never to write to her again. This isn't a separation, it's a divorce. I tell you, Pastor and Mrs. Nelson, I'm at heart a married man. I loved my children and wife. It's hard, so very hard, for since my mother and father are both dead now I'm all alone. I have no family. No one!"

Then his face brightened and he blurted out, "Will you be mother and dad to me?" And with that we were in each other's arms, our tears making answer to his cry and cementing a new tie for the three of us.

Some time later he asked Clarence with great seriousness, "Dad, would it be all right for me as a Christian to hope to marry again even with my wife alive? I long to begin a new home and family." I recalled then that letter and also told him that the rule of thumb for remarriage in our church was a "yes" to the innocent party where there had been sexual infidelity or where there was willful and permanent desertion. Such a marriage could have the blessing of the church.

Paul did marry again on his return to Taipei. His new wife was a widow, a committed Christian with a daughter. The two children born into that wedlock have been named "Clarence" and "Ruth." They are a happy family.

The "bread on the waters" theme as applied to Paul T. M. King has more than one side. It goes on and on. He gives himself wholeheartedly as a lay leader in Truth Church. He chaired the building committee in building a beautiful temple to the glory of God. His gift, says Clara Jones, is the sharpened sense of stewardship and he has been mightily used in wide church circles. He freely witnesses to the blessings he has known in his personal life.

For some years after returning to Taiwan Paul served the Premier as secretary and speech writer. He was immensely helpful in gathering material for important state papers. Sometimes this meant travel in the premier's retinue as they touched down at the various capitals across our world. One day we had a call from Blair House, the president's guest house. It was Paul and he was a guest there while his premier was on a state visit in Washington. You may be sure Paul was back that Sunday at old Augustana renewing friendships.

Are we selfish in telling how there was bread on the waters when our plane touched down in Taiwan? We were making our way to Dhahran, Saudi Arabia, after furlough in America. Paul had registered us as his guests at Hotel Imperial, surely the nicest hotel Clarence and I ever stayed in with its onyx grand staircase and storied carvings. Our spacious room had wainscot of white marble. Moreover there was a balcony looking out across the sprawling city to the mountains beyond. It made us want to pinch ourselves to ask, "Is it real or are we modern-day Alices in Wonderland?" Each morning Paul made a point of breakfasting with us before hurrying off to his office. Then a car and driver would be at the door with our great friend G. Nelson Yu (another Washington friend now head of the Bank of China and a Professor of Banking at the local university) to guide us to the special sights. We were driven to Madame Kai-shek's mountain retreat where she held her weekly Bible class. We stopped to see the mountain people whose dress and physiognomy reminded us so much of our American Indians. There was even a fabulous steam bath followed by a rest on straw woven couches.

Best of all was being asked to address a crowd of students on that Saturday night. Some had already said their "yes" to the Savior and others had come as seekers with open minds. These crowded the student hall and warmly welcomed what we had to say. Afterwards there was beautiful fellowship with eager and alert young Christians. Talk about bread cross the waters: Much of it was the fruit of the faithful sowing of beloved missionaries like Clara Jones, Victor and Evodia Swenson and others. I love to add here God's promise as found in Isaiah 32:20:

"Happy are you who sow beside many waters."

As I write these lines I have a letter from Paul before me. He is now secretary general of the Central Bank of China. The winds of change are blowing hard across this little island. It takes clear heads and skillful maneuvering to keep one's footing. But there's hope ahead with a new breed of leaders who daily look to God for guidance. They feed on the "hidden manna," the "true bread that is come into the world," even Jesus.

Children
Make Their Parents Grow

How can parents impartially write of their children? And yet when we think about the thousandfold return of bread, they do become Exhibit "A." It would be easy to look back on the mistakes one has made in the years of their rearing. But these we must leave with the Lord, and instead we find ourselves overwhelmed with gratitude for the amazing way he uses crumbs and returns them in a thousand loaves.

The thrill of an eternal soul wrapped in a red-faced little baby being placed in one's arms cannot be described! The responsibility for guiding that tiny life is another thing. The joy that each one has brought to us reminds us that "our cup runneth over."

And how different each one is! How proud Grandpa Youngdahl was because our firstborn was named Jonathan Clarence, so that his initials were J. C. like his granddad's! The little six-pound nine-ounce boy, 22 inches long thrived on his mother's milk given at four-hour intervals, plus lots of love. Early in his development Jon gave evidence of being his own man, and of loathing pretense. One day when he was three years old he had been watching his father before the mirror in the bathroom. This was before the days of the electric shaver, so Clarence pressed his face close to the mirror so as not to cut himself. Jon came into the kitchen and said, "Dad sure thinks he's good-looking, doesn't he?"

There was the time when we weakened and gave the boys Easter rabbits for pets. Dad built a hutch in the empty lot behind the parsonage on Magnolia Street. Often neighborhood children would cut across to get to school and they usually would stop to watch the bunnies. One day Jon came in sobbing to announce that the rabbits had been cruelly put to death by some sharp stick or other object. I'll never forget his cry as he protested: "The bunnies weren't hurting anyone! Why did these boys kill them?"

Later when he was older he came home from school with a swollen lip. We had tried to teach the children that you don't return evil for evil. (We never permitted play guns or toys suggesting violence.) When I asked our son what happened, he turned to me with a sheepish grin and said, "I turned the other lip!"

We were eager that our children get the true spirit of Christmas which at its heart is unselfish giving, and then to know the joy it brings. So our pre-Christmas conversation was what we could give to the Christ child for his birthday. But one day I weakened and took the boys over to Dayton's toy department. They were fascinated, especially by the electric trains. That night at our family prayer time five-year-old Jon prayed, "Dear Lord, if I get two trains for Christmas, help me to give one to the poor!"

That "twinkle in the eye" grew increasingly evident through the years. He was 10 years old when he pulled another little surprise on us. We had been attending a meeting and came home to find a note in large handwriting propped against a vase on the piano. It read, "Dad and Mom, awaken me for an important message when you get home." So we hurried upstairs to arouse our boy from deep sleep. I'll never forget the moment when his dad leaned over the bed and said, "Jon, what was the important message?" After a moment's wait for comprehension, he replied with a grin, "I just wanted to tell you that I love you!"

Through the years as the lad grew to be a man there developed a fine honed sense of indignation over injustice, over hypocrisy of all kinds. And with it the Christian grace and compassion and concern to address the needs of the oppressed and exploited. As chaplain on university campuses, he lent a sympathetic ear to the war protesters and was accredited with other chaplains by a college president as being in large part responsible for averting rioting and violence on the campus.

At the height of student indignation at the Kent State massacre and the American Vietnam policy, Jon quietly went to work. Getting the other chaplains with him they suggested both to the student leaders and to the administration that these meet together and by keeping the channels of communication open find common ground. It happened! There was a large rally. Students freely spoke their minds and the administration represented by its president and faculty heads gave a respectful ear. Promises were made about changes of school policy and with this the tensions began to relax. A huge rally on the green followed in candlelight when a litany of peace was joined in by all.

It was at that meeting in the university auditorium just when the shouting and angry outbursts were at their height that Jon saw a student whom he knew to be a ringleader for violence on the campus dart out into the night. Suspecting he might have arson in mind Jon followed him running through the night in and among the buildings. Jon was a jogger and couldn't be shaken. Finally the fellow turned to shout, "I know you, Nelson. Let me tell you something. You're a marked man. I've got four guys laying for you!"

Jon managed to persuade the fellow to come to the snack shop and talk over a cup of coffee. For two hours they rapped and by that time the blind rage that could very well have ended in the burning of a library or other buildings had subsided.

However most of Jon's efforts have a more constructive face:

the organizing of the community to launch a sheltered work-shop, seeing a high-rise, low-rent housing project for senior citizens and the poor; arranging for the confrontation of doctors to hear out the complaints of the aging that they were being shortchanged in health care.

Since moving to the campus in Seattle, Jon has found still other causes to champion. His indignation heats up over our abuse of Indian Treaty Rights on fishing, over refusal to grant amnesty to protesting draftees who couldn't stomach Vietnam. The shunting to one side of the aging and neglect of the mentally ill also is a deep concern to him, and he is always organizing groups from the campus to visit and cheer up these overlooked persons.

Whenever we can get away to visit Jon and Juni and family we haven't been settled in for long when Jon will say, "Folks, there's an old guy in the hospital I'd like to have you meet," or "Would you mind taking time to go with me to the retirees' high-rise? There are some friends there I promised a visit from you."

Perhaps family is as symbolic of "returned bread" as anything. Jon married a kindred spirit in breadth of heart and daring to live! Three lovely children were born to this marriage. When Kris, the eldest, was seven she announced to her grandparents, "We've decided to become consumers instead of producers." And so they began adopting! There are now eight in that family, with all shades of skin and hair. The last one, an eight-year-old boy from Korea, had been a foundling on the streets of Seoul at the tender age of a year-and-a-half. He had polio and was crippled from the waist down. Jon reports, "We don't have family quarrels; we have race riots in our home!" They have recently added a ninth child, a four-year-old boy from Vietnam who found love and security while awaiting the possibility of his Vietnamese mother coming to the U.S. Yesterday's letter describes a touching moment, as he writes:

> Last night a real human drama was played out in
> our kitchen. Hai's mother was on the telephone

having just arrived at Camp Pendleton, a refugee. She had gotten out first to the Philippines and then to Wake Island. Juni said she spoke excellent English and seemed very poised in the conversation. Anyway, we rushed out to the front where Hai was playing, and brought him to the phone. A kind of curious look flattened to amazement, then a big grin took over from all the corners of his face, and a couple of tears ran down his cheek. He was too moved and startled to respond. So after a bit Juni got back on the line, and Hai's mother asked if Hai had been at the phone. Juni described Hai's reaction to his mother encouraging her to urge Hai that he answer. Once again Hai was on, and this time he gave some assents audible to his mother. But he was still pretty well numbed and quiet by it all.

Anyway this morning he popped out of his bed and ran into the living room where I was sitting in the easy chair. He made a sign of an airplane up in the air and landing, and said, "Mama!" He'd got the picture, and we hope in the next few days his mother will have her papers processed and then be able to join him here. A New York Times reporter who'd befriended the mother had called yesterday from New Jersey and said among other things that Hai's mother is a delightful person, an English teacher for the older Holt Orphanage children. She herself is an orphan with no family.

I tease Juni that we may just have adopted our first grandchild-and-mother set.

What greater joy could any parents know, what greater return from the sharing of the Bread of Life, than that their children should find their fulfillment in serving others.

I see how children make their parents grow.

I Like Her Crazy

One year and 11 days after Jonathan's birth, our son David was put in my arms. There were those who lifted their eyebrows and said, "Another baby so soon?" Maybe his birth announcement will tell you just how we felt as parents!

THE PARSONAGE KID

When people heard I was coming,
    They almost blew their lid;
They said: "Poor Mrs. Nelson!
    There'll be another parsonage kid."

But Mommy and Daddy just chuckled;
    They were as pleased as punch instead.
They rejoiced that the Lord had given them
    Another parsonage lad.

My name is David Theodore,
    Jonathan is my brother's name.
We hope that we will be friends like
    The boys of biblical fame!

No matter what others are saying,
    The welcome I've had is not hid;
And I am very grateful
    To be another parsonage kid.

He was a breech baby, and even the doctor felt the presence of a higher power, because he came into the world unharmed and healthy. We had planned that if the expected one were a boy, he would be named David for we wanted the biblical relationship of our two sons' namesakes to be theirs also. And that's the way it became.

The technically difficult birth presaged some of the narrow escapes that have since been David's experiences. Out at our cabin (Nelson's Koja) on Sand Lake, the children would gather on a neighbor's raft for their swimming fun. Often they would play King of the Mountain, the idea being to see who could persist in shoving everyone else off the raft. Dave had a special scheme in mind, so unobserved he slipped under the raft. His idea was to come up on an unexpected side and pull someone off. He miscalculated the raft's edge and instead came up sharply underneath it, splitting his head open. Someone by mere chance saw blood in the water and Dave was pulled out from underneath, rushed to the doctor, and had 14 stitches put in his head.

In the early years at Sand Lake we had to get our drinking water at a neighbor's pump. Dave and Jon went there to fill our bucket. Somehow Dave's thumb got caught in the pump's mechanism, and he came running home with his fingernail torn off.

I treasure the remembrance of his chubby, upturned face the day I decided we'd have an outing, school or no school. Their pastor father had been so busy that there had been little time for family fun. So on a beautiful Monday morning in spring when the children came down for breakfast I announced they weren't going to school that day; that we were going out to our lake cottage. This was sheer heresy for a mother who was a former schoolteacher! They all pitched in to pack our lunch, and as we were going out the door, I turned to Dave at my side and said, "You've got the craziest mother!" With a big grin, he dimpled back at me, "I like her crazy!"

I remember the night we turned home at dusk from some calls to find Dave in the gutter by the roadside with his arms around our dead cocker spaniel "Puffer." A neighbor had accidentally run over the dog, and consoling a tender lad about his loss wasn't easy. His little body was wracked with sobs. The grief was somewhat assuaged when we were able to pick up a tiny puppy who was reported to be cocker. "Ole" turned out to be an "International Harvester," as our boys put it, but he was no less loved for all that.

One day in his early years Dave had been naughty, and I had to punish him. Before I sent him into his room, I said to him, "You know, Dave, I still love you even when you're naughty, even though you make me very unhappy when you misbehave. And God loves you too although he hates your naughtiness!" There was no sound from his "isolation room" for some time. Then I heard the patter of little feet. He looked up at me and said, "Mummy, I love myself when I'm naughty, too!"

He was always a generous lad, and wanted to give more than to receive. He still is that way, only more so.

At college the children all helped work their way through. Dave and Jon had jobs in the town restaurant and often worked until midnight. An unforgettable Mother's Day remembrance stems from this experience. The dishwasher in the cafe was a little widow who had no family. Often the boys would take her home in their secondhand "heap." On this particular Mother's Day I received a note from them which said, "Mother, instead of sending you a corsage this year, we knew you'd be happy if we give Mrs. Olson a flower and take her to dinner on Mother's Day!"

Bread on the waters! What mother could ask for more?

Dave interrupted his seminary years to spend six months at a Hebrew Institute in Jerusalem. This was a "window to the world" experience for him. Coming through war-devastated Europe by train on his return was to him a traumatic experience that burned deep into his soul. I don't think he ate anything all the way through Yugoslavia, he was so crushed by the human need he saw on every side.

When he was ready to be ordained, he put as his first preference an inner-city church. Bread on the waters? He had thrilled to our Washington experience where our church was involved with what we called "Operation One Mile." Every home in a mile radius was visited by our members to invite all who had no church affiliation to worship with us. David saw the miracle of Christ's love breaking racial barriers firsthand.

Army people have a saying, "Ask for an assignment to Alaska and get sent to Wake Island." Seminarians didn't always get what they asked for so Dave was sent to Country Club Hills south of Chicago at about 196th and Cicero. After some 900 survey calls, he gathered a group to organize "House of Prayer" congregation. At first they met in a school and later a lovely sanctuary was built. Then there came the opportunity for his inner-city work. In what was Garfield Park, at Bethel Lutheran Church, he became pastor of a congregation. The very day he drove in to prepare his first sermon, rioting was already under way. His sister was in the front seat with him and he had to push her down under the cowl as a huge stone came through his car window.

As he walked those streets and lived into the lives of his people he was overwhelmed by the injustices and the seeming hopelessness of the ghetto trap. He sought counsel with two other pastors in the neighborhood. Soon the three joined forces to launch C A M (Christian Action Ministry). But the story from here on would be a book in itself. After 10 years of growth there are now more than 12 churches involved. Such economically redemptive services as Job Placement, Consumers' Protection, Sheltered Work Shop, Second Chance Academy, Bethel C A M Christian Elementary School, Child Development Centers (nine at this writing). A whole city block has been set aside for a Human Development Center to house a nursing home, medical clinics, child development center, and a penthouse church for all faiths to use. This miracle goes by the name of "The Ash Flower Operation." Only God's blessings on committed lives could be the answer! Yes, and the fearless courage that has been willing to take physical beatings without once fighting back.

One day as he was coming out of C A M headquarters on Madison Avenue a woman screamed, "Get those guys! They've stolen my money!" She had just cashed her weekly check of $125 at the money exchange. Dave saw two young men running away and what did he do but give pursuit. It was summer and warm, so he was coatless, and his clergy shirt was much in evidence. After they had crossed Goldblatt's Parking Lot the two thieves separated. Surely the Lord guided him in the choice of which to continue pursuing. He dogged the one who ran across the lawn of a senior citizens' home. Many of the occupants were sitting around on benches, and Dave chuckles when he recalls how they called out, "Get him, Preach! Get him!" The thief charged between the two buildings, little realizing that he was headed down a cul-de-sac. Now Dave was upon him but the thief shouted, "Here's the money. Let me go!" And with that he flung down the fist of bills and when Dave stooped to gather them he lost himself in the crowd on the sidewalk. Dave was thrilled to return the whole of her $125 to the amazed woman. In her astonishment and gratitude, she asked, "Didn't he pull his gun on you like he did on me?" That was when Dave realized that the Lord had led him to follow not only the one with the money but also the one who was unarmed.

His little parsonage has been broken into seven times! Now the congregation has put bars on the windows so when we visit there Clarence calls it, "Fortress David."

Was it because of David's passion for the deprived and downtrodden that sent him into the slums as a shepherd and caused him to be chosen to serve the national church as spearheading "Love Compels Action" that Augustana College of Rock Island, Illinois, conferred upon him the D.D. Honoris Causa in 1973? At 38 he had lived a lot of life and it heartens one to know that the church at large would recognize this.

He has served as chairman of our national church "World

Hunger" and "Love Compels Action" appeals. It all fits together! It's the generosity of a Christ-filled heart that responds to human need—everywhere!

I see how children make their parents grow.

Bread upon the waters.

She Spreads the Bread
in Indonesia

Clarence grew up in a family of seven boys. There had been a sister, Ruth, but at the tender age of eight she died of diphtheria. Although I had three sisters, there were six boys in my family. My brother Ben, the economist-sociologist, had it statistically figured out that our chances of having a girl were mighty slim.

You can imagine the joy, then, when three years after David's arrival, our daughter Elizabeth was born. Writing her name makes me smile. The Lord had tapped my mother on the shoulder in the interim between the two babies, so I much wanted our lass to carry her name. Her daddy thought it would be better that she carry her mother's name, Ruth. We thought we had compromised with the combination Elizabeth Ruth. Imagine my astonishment at the baptismal font, to hear my husband as the officiating pastor say, "I now baptize you, Ruth Elizabeth . . . "

He claims it to have been a mere slip of the tongue! Martin Luther says we should put the most charitable construction on all our neighbor's action, but I still wonder!

Anyhow, her little brothers soon solved the problem. They couldn't quite manage Elizabeth, so it came out Bizabeth, and then shortly became just Biz! And that has been her identification in the family ever since.

Early in life she indicated she had a mind of her own. She was two years old when she wanted to sleep in her dolly's cradle. It was too short for her so we insisted she go into her own bed. She seemed contented enough as we stood around her bedside singing our evening prayer. (Each of the children had been a part of this ritual from the day they arrived home from the hospital!)

> Jesus tender shepherd, hear me.
> Bless thy little lamb tonight.
> Through the darkness be thou near me;
> Keep me safe 'til morning light.
>
> All this day thy love has kept me,
> And I thank thee for thy care.
> Thou hast warmed me, fed and clothed me,
> Listen to my evening prayer.
>
> May my sins be all forgiven;
> Bless the friends I love so well.
> Take me, Lord, at last to heaven,
> Safely there with thee to dwell.

I said she seemed contented enough! Well, little did I know what was going on in that active mind! We had a friend come in to be with the children that night because there was a meeting we both had to attend. We didn't call them baby-sitters! We couldn't have afforded one. It was in the "great depression." When we returned, she reported how good the children had been and now all was quiet.

As was our custom before we retired we went in to check each chick. Imagine our surprise and concern when we found Biz' bed empty! We searched the house looking under the beds, in the closets, and every place we could think of. Finally I saw the cradle crib in a far corner behind a chair. Sure enough, there was our little lady, crunched together where a doll should be, and sleeping soundly! Now that's determination at an early age.

I mentioned Dave's many accidents! Well, I think Biz had him beat. As a very little girl in St. Paul she was watching a neighbor burn leaves. One flew up and caught fire on her overalls. It was her small brother Jon's quick thinking that put out that fire on her pantlets with his bare hands. But already the tender flesh had been severely burned. And I remember rocking her and singing, "I went to the animal fair," to divert her mind from the searing pain while we awaited the doctor's arrival. Imagine! Doctors did make house calls back in those days! But now today I would know that the best remedy during that wait would have been to get running ice water on it.

The scars are still to be seen on her knee; and there are scars on her ankle. When riding handlebars with one of her brothers, her foot caught in the front spokes. The flesh was torn open to the bone. Then there was the time she was riding with her Sunday school teacher on Duluth's Skyline Drive. Biz was in the back seat, and the door wasn't locked. As the car swung around a corner Biz pressed against the door, opening the lock and so was hurtled headlong onto the loose gravel and cinders of the roadway. On her forehead, if you look closely, you'll find the scar. And there's another on her upper lip where two stitches had to be taken when as a three-year-old she caught her lip on the corner of the car door as she tried to climb in!

All this was capped with rheumatic fever at the age of 12— when for a year she was bedridden. I learned to take temperatures, register the pulse, and give rubdowns. Her sixth grade teacher discovered her art talent. How grateful we are to that instructor who sought the best in each of her pupils. School was easy for Biz. Without her Duluth teacher knowing it until the end of the year, she had doubled on grades. Two grades were taught in one room so Biz would finish her work quickly and then do the other grade's assignment as well.

Recently I met one of her teachers. She recounted the time I had come to Lincoln School for the Christmas program. I was to tell the story of "Why the Chimes Rang!" When the class returned to its room, this teacher asked for their reactions. One boy raised his hand and when called upon said, "Biz' mother can tell a story almost as good as Biz can!" Had Biz' skill at story telling been sharpened by the radio Bible Story Hour which I and the children carried through each week for three years?

Biz admired her brothers so much that she wanted to dress and act like a boy. It was a great day when she wanted to buy a pair of silk stockings! Yet at heart she was always the genuine American girl!

There was the time I was having "a woman to woman" talk with her and explaining some of the inconveniences of menstruation and the necessity for the greatest care in personal hygiene. She listened with grave attention as I concluded, "It seems like a lot of monkey business, but it's God's way of making it possible for us to have lovely little babies!" Her response is unforgettable, "Yes, and look at the men! All they get is whiskers!"

She won a national prize in our church young people's organization when just 13 for a poster she had designed. The prize was $10, a lot of money in those days for a schoolgirl. We wondered how she would spend it. We needn't have. She had heard about Chinese orphans, and the entire check was dispatched to that cause. This really turned out to be a symbol of her value norms.

In her senior high school year in Washington she was named "Girl of the Year." The Washington Post gave that honor a half-page spread! She was a fine student, but more than that she loved people and related to them. Her social life was in her church youth group, but sometimes we wondered if she felt she was missing out at school. Some of the parties had a reputation for being wild.

One night as I was retiring, I heard sobbing from her room. This was very unusual as she was a happy girl. I went in and asked her what was the matter! She responded, "It's nothing, Mother! It's not important. You need your sleep!"

117

I knew I shouldn't force a confidence so I went to bed to pray. I heard my Lord say, "Have no anxiety in anything . . . " The next morning in our family devotions as we took our turns about the breakfast table before the children were off to school, Biz' prayer was "Please God, give me a long look and a right sense of values. And help me not to be concerned about adiaphora!" That was one of her clergyman father's words for trivial things! How often I've thought of that prayer.

Like the others, she worked her way through college. Between her junior and senior years she became part of the University of Minnesota program called S P A N (Student Project for Amity Among Nations). She chose the field of mental health and went to South Africa for her observation and study. She was appalled and disturbed by the apartheid practices. Then she chose to spend her "free" week with our missionaries in Tanzania. While there she talked to a girls' school. The missionary in charge wrote us, "When Biz had finished, the girls came to me and said, 'She must come back! She belongs here!' "

She didn't go back to Tanzania, but she did go to the islands of Southeast Asia. After she finished college at the age of 20, she did social work in Anoka for one year to get money to pay off her college debt. Then she offered herself to the Board of World Missions of her church. Of the openings suggested, she chose to go to Indonesia to teach English in the Nommensen Seminary in Siantar of Sumatra. There she met a German theologian, a fellow teacher. They were married in the Cathedral of Stuttgart, and returned as a team to Indonesia. To them were born Karl and Inge, and this family of ours is now in Jakarta where Walle teaches in the Ecumenical Seminary.

And Biz? Besides running a household that is always running over with guests, she gives herself freely in the government leprosarium. With American and Australian women as fellow volunteers, she has helped to start a rehabilitation center where the men raise ducks, and the women weave and do artwork as a means of self-support. A library is now functioning through their efforts and books and reading materials and an attendant are provided by funds from friends.

There were so many little street boys coming to their door for food and clothing that a Street Boys' Home became a crying need. Such a home has since been started. Biz is also busy in church school workshops, helps write curriculums, and puts her hand to teaching teachers. Her love spills out to everyone!

This is the girl who was bedridden for a year immobilized by rheumatic fever!

I see how children make their parents grow.

Give Me
a Clean Blackboard, Lord!

Three years after Biz' advent, Mary came on the scene. A wee little lass, she spent her first days in an incubator. Yet when she was two weeks old, in a basket she attended her foster sister's graduation from Gustavus Adolphus College, so quickly did she make up for a slow start.

Her intuitive theological perception, even as a child, amazed us. The aging mother of one of our friends was dying of cancer. All older women were "grandmas" to our children. One night $3\frac{1}{2}$-year-old Mary's prayer was, "Dear God, please bless Grandma Anderson, and I kinda think you ought to take her home to be with you, Lord. She's suffered so much. But then, you know what's best, and she's with you now and she'll be with you then, so it really doesn't make any difference."

On her second day of school, (her teacher had asked her to help clean the blackboards after the first day) she prayed at our morning prayer time, "Please God, give me a clean blackboard today, and help me to do the writing." We came across her confirmation Bible and found it so underlined and annotated as to give away its constant use.

She had a mind of her own, too! As husband and wife we often chuckled about how two plus two makes four. Both of us can be "stubborn Swedes" and the addition can become in one's children a "Rock of Gibraltar."

We had wanted all our children to know the joy of music, both the creating of it and the enjoying of it. I remember the time Mary didn't want to practice her lesson, but her stubborn mother persisted. So the girl sat down on the piano bench sullenly, and pounded the keys mercilessly. It was horrible! I came in from the kitchen and suggested maybe we'd better pray about her practicing!

We had daily experiences in our family to show how prayer can change the climate. I would not have dared to propose this otherwise. Surely she wouldn't dare defy God! But her rebellious attitude persisted, and she dragged her feet as we knelt to talk with God. What a temptation was mine at that point! I wanted to preach to Mary in that prayer, but the Holy Spirit was working. I simply prayed: "Please, God, help me to be the kind of mother you want me to be, and help us as a family to do what you would want us to do." Then I arose and went to the kitchen. Oh, don't think that I wasn't tempted to try to be God's helper at that moment, and say, "Now, Mary, you go and practice the piano!" But again the Holy Spirit took over and made me to know I must trust his gentle pressure on Mary's heart.

It took a half an hour before I was to hear results. Then beautifully Mary took up the practicing again! Later that night Mary came to me and said, "Mom, forgive me. I don't know why I act that way! I'm sorry!"

We still have some of the little blue slips she had hidden around the house just before her return to college after vacation. There was one under the mirror on the dresser; one in the bathroom on the shelf; another pinned on our bed pillow. Here are samples: "Thanks, Dad and Mom, for the great vacation! How blest I am!" Another: "I'll be praying for you as we move across the miles, and will be secure in knowing your prayers will be surrounding me!"

What bread to come back from teaching a little child the reality of prayer and to know the God who answers!

Mary took her junior year of college in Germany under a program of Wayne State University, where students crossed the waters to do their studying in another language. She studied in German, among other things a course in English Literature in Munich. It seemed such a paradox to me! She lived in the International Ecumenical House (costing a mere pittance) and here the windows to the world that had been her experience in Washington as we gave hospitality to people from many lands got flung wide open for her too. Her correspondence still embraces the world, including some meaningful relationships in Eastern Europe. Between school terms, she spent four weeks traveling with student groups by train to Russia. Because of her proficiency in German she was identified as a student from that country. She smuggled in 12 Russian Bibles, some wrapped in her underwear and some in her duffel bag concealed under other garments. Her clandestine meeting with a Moscow pastor to deliver these was a story contained in one of her interesting letters. She made it to Leipzig for a Christian Youth Conference, where behind drawn shades young students studied the Bible together. She wrote home about the time she got on the train to leave these new-found friends, how she wept copiously at the separation and the bleak future that seemed to be the fate of those from whom she had just parted and learned to love.

When we met her in New York, she looked for all the world like a refugee. She had given away everything she owned except the clothes on her back.

"Ignorance is bliss" is an old saying, and I guess this is specially true for parents. We didn't know until later some of the narrow escapes she had. There was the time when she was to meet her girlfriend in France. This friend owned a motorcycle and they were to visit Switzerland together. They had agreed to meet at a certain building near the border of Belgium. Mary's boat had been delayed in its channel crossing so when she came to the appointed place, the building had been demolished! Upon closer scrutiny Mary did find a note attached to the one standing wall which read: "Dear Mary, I waited 24 hours. What happened? Meet me in Brussels at the Youth Hostel." By this time Mary had used up her slim resources and was depending on her friend to supply her temporarily. She was bone-weary and hungry and night was coming on. She started out walking, hoping to hitch a ride! But the roads were empty. As night crept on, wearying took over and she knew she simply couldn't make it any further. She found a little railroad station and slipped into its warmth. Stretching out on a bench, she was soon fast asleep. Rudely she was awakened by a lantern flashing in her face. A black-robed man stood over her. He was the station master. He made her to understand she'd have to get out. He had to lock up the building. Blearily she wondered where she'd go. When she stepped outside, she saw a dim light a few blocks away. Arriving at this ray of hope she stumbled in and found it to be a tavern. She ordered a cup of coffee—and immediately fell asleep with her head on the counter. Then she felt a gentle nudge and heard a voice in broken English, "You're tired. I have a room for you!" She relates that by this time her senses were dulled, and it never occurred to her that she was in any kind of danger.

It was like heaven to slip between the clean covers of the bed. The next morning there was a knock at the door, and the same friendly voice said, "I have some breakfast ready." She explained to him that she was out of money. Then he told her, "When the Americans came in to help us in the war, they were wonderful to my family and really kept us alive. I've always wanted a chance to say thank you to an American!"

Bread upon the waters!

Another time she was hitchhiking and was offered a ride in the cab of a truck. She had a feeling the driver didn't have the best of intentions! He turned to her and asked, "Aren't you afraid to be alone like this?"

She replied, "I'm not alone!"

He said, "What do you mean?" Her response was, "God is with me!" She described the reaction was as if a garment of asbestos had been wrapped around her.

Finishing college at 20, she received a scholarship toward an experimental cram program at Brown University which would permit her to receive an M.A. and a teacher's certificate in one year. She offered herself to the church and was assigned to the Ashira Girls' School in Moshi, Tanzania. After an orientation quarter at the Chicago Lutheran School of Theology, she began a two-year assignment there on the slopes of the Kilimanjaro Mountain.

Her teaching experience in this rapidly developing country was deeply fulfilling. The young African girls were so eager to get on with their learning that they'd gobble up books even studying after the electricity had been turned off, clustered like moths around that last lamp. Through good friends in Saudi Arabia we were able to supply her with a number of textbooks (the affluence at that school permitted frequent changes). Also through friends she was instrumental in gathering what was to be the beginning of a good library. These two years she counts as some of her greatest.

But she was reading of riots and burning back in the states as U.S. blacks were trying to break out of the confining trap that skin color had made for them. So she returned to the states to put herself at the place of greatest need. She became a part of C A M (Christian Action Ministry) operation in West Garfield Park, Chicago, where her brother David had just become the pastor of Bethel. Under Mary's guidance the C A M Academy (a second-chance high school for dropouts) has developed. It has received national attention for its redemptive work with those considered uneducable by the public schools. Accredited by the Illinois State Board of Education, it now has the record of 65% of its graduating youth going on to higher education. During this time she has worked for and received her Ph.D. in Urban Education from Antioch College.

When we lived in Chicago we received a telephone call as we were retiring. It was from our son Dave. "Mary has been beaten," he said. "She's at the hospital. We don't know how seriously."

124

That was a memorable ride, a praying ride, as we tore from Chicago's South Side down to Lake Shore Drive to the Eisenhower Expressway to the Community Hospital at West Garfield Park. There we discovered she had been moved to another hospital since no doctor was at hand to administer to her. When we protested saying, "Oh, no!" Dave answered, "But folks, this is what my people get all the time." So it was over to St. Anne's where Dave had taken her by ambulance. For this conveyance you have to pay $40 in cash ready! There in the emergency room her father hurried to her side. Mary's eyes opened momentarily from the coma she was in, and he whispered, "Mary, you'll just have to move away from this area!" Her reply before slipping back into unconsciousness, "Dad, I'll be back at my desk at C A M before this week is out." The doctors had to put 13 stitches in her head. She was bleeding internally from the brutal kicking with leather-heeled shoes and her arms and chest were one big blur of purple from bruising. She did make it to her desk with her head swathed in bandages just as she had predicted.

There she pours out her life, meeting with Foundations, lobbying at the State Legislature for money grants so sorely needed in this depressed area, speaking to countless groups as she pleads for people to be concerned about the causes of society's infections, instead of just standing by with Band-Aid remedies.

In Bethel Church she teaches Sunday school and participates in all activities, and even substitutes at the organ when emergencies arise. She often writes the festival programs for the church school.

And her apartment is constantly filled with a variety of people who share her warm hospitality and are refreshed with genuine warm friendship.

An avid reader herself, she is constantly feeding us books to help us be aware of the scene today, a scene that so desperately needs the impact of concerned, committed Christians.

The little girl who prayed, "Give me a clean blackboard

125

today" has come a long way and has found tremendous fulfillment as a channel for the love of the One to whom she so earnestly committed herself at confirmation.

I see how children make their parents grow.